A VICTORIAN SCRAPBOOK

BY CYNTHIA HART AND JOHN GROSSMAN
TEXT BY PRISCILLA DUNHILL

WORKMAN PUBLISHING • NEW YORK

To our grandparents and parents

Sylvia and John Herd, Nellie and Harry Hart
Theo and Herbert Hart
Pearl and Ernest Howell, Matilda and Frank Grossman
Ruth and John Grossman
Emma and George Christman, Zella and Wayne Smith
Miriam and Carlton Smith

The photographic illustrations were created by Cynthia Hart and recorded on film by
Steven Tex. All the paper ephemera circa 1820–1920 is from The John Grossman
Collection of Antique Images. Priscilla Dunhill provided the text.

Library of Congress Cataloging-in-Publication Data
Hart, Cynthia. A Victorian scrapbook.
1. Great Britain—Social life and customs—19th century.
2. United States—Social life and customs—19th century.
3. Printed ephemera—Great Britain.
4. Printed ephemera—United States.
I. Grossman, John. II. Dunhill, Priscilla. III. Title.
DA550.H36 1989   941.081   89-40373   ISBN 0-89480-620-3

Typeset by BPE Graphics

Workman Publishing Company, Inc.
708 Broadway
New York, New York 10003

Printed in Japan
First printing October 1989
10 9 8 7 6 5 4 3 2 1

For their generous loans of Victorian jewelry, dolls and other antique objects for our photographs, we thank Dorene Burger (Treasures from the Past, Antiques by Dorene, New York City), Susan Hoy (Susan's Storeroom, San Anselmo, California), Rochelle Mendle (Oakland, California) and Arlene Kahn (Irving Place Antiques, New York City).

For his photographic expertise and unfailing good humor, we thank Steven Tex.
For her advice and encouragement, we thank Nancy Lindemeyer.
For her early-morning forays into the flower market, we thank Petra Koencke (Petra's Gallery of Flowers, Sausalito, California).
For their dedication and goodwill, we thank the research librarians at the San Francisco Public Library.
For his knowledge of the history of chromolithography, we thank Jay T. Last.
For his personal contributions to American lithography, we thank George Schlegel III.
For their cheerful support, we thank Carolyn Grossman, Harumi Ando, Elisa Davidson, Pat Upton, Ciba Vaughn, Molly Blayney, Gloria Somers, Roslyn Tunis, Sharyn Prentiss, Thomas Ando-Hart, Joanne Lees, Janet Saghatelian, and everyone at The Gifted Line.
For having preserved the family and business ephemera that ultimately found its way to this book, we thank many, many anonymous individuals.
For locating, securing and offering fine ephemera over the years, we thank the many antique paper and collectibles dealers.
For giving form and substance to the study of ephemera, we thank the Ephemera Society of America, Schoharie, New York, and its president, William F. Mobley.
For his enthusiasm and open-minded view of publishing, we thank Peter Workman.
For his creative prowess, we thank Paul Hanson.
For her personal commitment to excellence, we thank our editor Sally Kovalchick.
For their graphic design contributions, we thank Lisa Hollander and Karen Petersen.
For her work as "wordsmith," we thank Lynn Strong.
For helping in so many other ways, we thank everyone at Workman Publishing.

CONTENTS

Working with the antique images in this book gave me a rare look into the day-to-day lives of women and men of generations ago. I saw their most passionate concerns, causes and dreams, still at the core of our lives today. Each wisp of fragile paper that I touched had miraculously captured a moment and had used its beauty and subtle powers to ensure its own safekeeping.

I am thankful to John Grossman for having the foresight, discerning eye and perseverance to build his magnificent collection, and for his generosity in opening its treasures to me. It is Priscilla Dunhill's "magic pencil" that unleashed the stories hidden behind the ephemera.

Our book will let you peek directly into the Victorian era and share its glory. You will find here a tribute to the good and beautiful side of life — may it touch your heart and bring you joy.

Cynthia Hart

Victorian ladies and their children, busily filling albums with the minor printed paper artifacts of daily life that otherwise would have been tossed out, inadvertently created an important record of their era. Some albums are works of art, beautifully arranged by young women of means using "scrap" purchased from fancy stationers. Others, from humbler homes, boast clippings, discards and advertising giveaways of local merchants.

I have been endlessly fascinated by the richness of life, the ideals, the sentiments and the beauty expressed in these old images. Cynthia Hart has arranged them into exquisite compositions. Priscilla Dunhill has written an evocative text inspired by them. It is our hope that new generations will continue to be charmed by them through this book.

We are all indebted to the "savers" who over the years just couldn't bring themselves to throw out "that old paper stuff in Grandma's trunk."

Today, block-long presses churn out printed paper ephemera by the millions. How much of this will survive a hundred years from now to give future generations a glimpse of our own daily lives? What are you doing with all those old Christmas cards? And the junk mail? And the frozen-food cartons?

John Grossman

Brilliantly colored birds on an uncut sheet of scrap from Germany, dated 1890. Because of their rarity, uncut sheets are most prized by collectors.

INTRODUCTION

For a hundred years, the brilliantly colored images reproduced in A VICTORIAN SCRAPBOOK have been tucked away, forgotten or preserved in private collections. These bright bits—scraps, they were called in Victorian times—leap from the page and stretch across the century to connect us with a golden time, a gentler time, a time spangled with beauty and innocence, the time of our great-grandmothers. Today these images, still as fresh and immediate as gossip over the backyard fence, are called antique paper ephemera. Originally intended for temporary use and enjoyment, then often discarded, they were reproduced by the early painstaking process of chromolithography, which simply means "printing in colors." After centuries of black ink on white paper, chromolithography intoxicated the world with its lush printed hues, transforming the look of trade and calling cards, valentines, wedding and birth announcements, cigar box labels, calendars and chromos—pretty scenes meant to be hung on the wall.

Chromolithography had a dazzling, meteoric life, appearing on the American scene about 1840 and vanishing during the third

decade of the twentieth century. During those nearly 100 years, anonymous commercial artists worked directly on Bavarian limestone printing slabs first brought to America by European printers who emigrated to New York, Philadelphia and Boston in the 1830s. Working from a finely detailed watercolor painting by another artist, the highly skilled lithographic artist analyzed the painting for its basic colors. Drawing in black, in reverse image, on separate stones for each color, he visualized in his head how the colors would overprint to re-create the original painting. The many stones were then printed in sequence, with astonishingly accurate registration. The edition completed, the images were ground off the stones, and their surfaces prepared for the next job.

The lithography part of the process, invented by Aloys Senefelder in 1798 in Bavaria, worked on the principle that oil and water do not mix: the images drawn in a greasy ink on the stone picked up the printing inks, while the remaining surface of the stone, covered with a thin film of water, did not. The result, typically printed from eight to twelve stones: layered colors, often embossed and gilded as well. By the end of the century, with the advent of mass advertising, mass magazines, and a four-color photomechanical printing process, labor-intensive chromolithography was no longer viable. The vivid hues, the depth and luminescence of Victorian ephemera will not pass our way again.

Cigar labels, representing as they did the heroes, heroines and fantasies of the American male, provide an incisive and delightful window on nineteenth-century history. The color veracity of the chromolithographic process is evident by comparing the two images of Liberty Light: the lower one is the original watercolor art, a rarity, from which the upper image was produced. The other two labels are also watercolor art.

Artists worked directly on the lithographic stones. The three shown here, weighing between twenty-five and thirty-five pounds, were required to make a single color for three different cigar labels.

HOME SWEET HOME

VICTORIA THE QUEEN

THE SAINTLINESS OF
MOTHERHOOD

CHILDHOOD
PLEASURES

An English commemorative card of Prince Albert and Queen Victoria's wedding in 1840.

Her Majesty, Victoria, by the grace of God, United Kingdom of Britain and Ireland, Queen, Defender of the Faith, Empress of India.

"*Victoria's reign may so stamp her influence . . . promoting the highest and best interests of virtue, learning, social happiness and national improvement of the period in which she flourishes, that history shall speak of it as her own.*"

—SARAH HALE, *editor of Godey's Lady's Book,* the American *homemaker's bible, on the eve of Victoria's accession to the throne*

Victoria's beloved consort, Prince Albert of Saxe-Coburg Gotha, in his late thirties.

In 1837, the year Victoria became Queen of England, a steadying moral influence was much needed on both sides of the Atlantic. England was reeling from the demoralizing reign of the demented King George III and from his licentious sons, who were Victoria's uncles. None of the King's surviving progeny had produced a legitimate heir to the throne, always cause for uneasiness in the British Empire. America was fumbling with expansion under the rough-hewn leadership of the fiery and often crude Andrew Jackson, the first president to be born west of the Appalachians and the first to use his office to make blatant political deals. Accustomed to presidents drawn from the aristocracy, Americans were wary, their confidence frayed, their sensibilities shocked.

Britain and America yearned for gentility and refinement. And Alexandrina Victoria, a "heaven-sent figure of youth and innocence," just under five feet tall, provided it. This slip of a girl, her small, plump fingers laden with rings, would be the moral and spiritual power that guided both nations for the next sixty-four years. Affectionate, industrious, an adoring wife and dutiful mother, she became a global model of domestic felicity. She and Prince Albert, her handsome and impeccably stuffy consort, sang rollicking rounds at his beloved organ in Windsor Castle and romped with their offspring at Balmoral, the family's newly

Ivory and sterling-silver baby rattles were often given as christening gifts.

purchased estate in Scotland. Even though she was Albert's sovereign and queen, she showed herself to be obedient and submissive with him—a message not lost on the wives of the English-speaking world.

If Victoria was the bedrock of morality, Motherhood was the crowning jewel in her tiara. As a "companion and helper in the work of civilization and Christian progress," a Victorian mother was expected to nourish the intellectual, spiritual and physical well-being of her flock, cheerfully and within the means provided by her husband. Resourcefulness, industry, good manners—these were the requisites of this domestic saint.

Poetry, novels and the pulpit gave a clear-eyed vision of the sacredness of her task. "She is to rear all under her care to lay up treasures, not on earth, but in heaven," intoned the powerful persuader *The American Woman's Home*. Further, the editors promised, "those who train immortal minds are to reap the fruit of their labor through eternal ages." As spiritual guardian, the Victorian mother bathed her children in the pure light of her piety

Cuddle and love me,
    cuddle and love me,
Crows the mouth of coral pink,
Oh the bald head, and oh the
    sweet lips,
And oh the sleepy eyes that
    wink!

—Christina Rossetti

AMITIÉ

"**K**indness and love is the chief glory of woman . . . her scepter and her crown. It is the sword with which she conquers and the charm with which she captivates."
—Mary Melendy, M.D., in Maiden, Wife and Mother, 1901

Souvenir d'Amitié

BOOK-MARK

MOTHER'S LOVE
FOR
BABY
PRACTICALLY APPLIED
RELIEVES SUFFERING AND
SMILES & SUNSHINE
FOLLOW.

This pastel portrait of three children on a trade card served two purposes: as an advertisement for Dr. Hand's Remedies for Crying and Sickly Children and as a bookmark.

A die-cut scrap of mother and child captures the essence of Victorian motherhood. Revered as the moral and spiritual guardians of the nation's children, mothers were also, at times, pampered.

and self-sacrifice. Her husband—mover, shaker, builder of roads, bridges and empires—had no time for the subtleties of right and wrong. Should prosperity look with divine favor upon him, hers was a divine mission worthy of it. She brought up her daughters to be as virtuous and marriageable as possible and taught her sons to honor the "sweet earnest feeling of ambition."

On becoming a mother, labeled by Queen Victoria as "the shadow side of marriage," the homemaking manuals of the mid-1800s fell eerily silent. For all a young bride knew, babies were deposited on chimney pots by storks or brought in the doctor's black bag; one fantasy explained that little boys sprang from cabbages, little girls from roses. Not until the christening did the home magazines chirp forth again: a silver rattle or mug was a proper gift for the infant, and it was acceptable to serve champagne at the christening tea, accompanied by almond macaroons, chocolate glacé biscuits, and pound cake cut in small pieces.

The Victorian mother's home was her glory: a symbol to the world of her husband's industry, his unflagging devotion, and her

Trade cards, colorful, sprightly, pocket-sized advertisements, were given out at point of purchase. They were collected, swapped and often pasted into scrapbooks. As spontaneous cheap throwaways, not taken seriously, they record an immediate and vivid picture of the daily life and aspirations of nineteenth-century America.

God-given opportunity to create a peaceful, safe haven for him and her children. Building a home of one's own was an aspiration of all classes. Couples eagerly poured over architectural pattern books. According to taste and pocketbook, they added a Gothic window here, a Queen Anne tower there, a cupola or two. In a final act of ebullience, they wrapped their dream house with gingerbread jigsaw bought by the yard.

With a passion for the ornate, Victorians covered their front parlors with floral wallpapers and stuffed them with tasseled velvet chairs, horsehair sofas, lace-covered tables and bric-a-brac. They filled whatnot shelves—a fad that originated with Queen Victoria—with keepsakes or collections of wax flowers, shells or geological specimens. *The American Woman's Book* suggested that such collections be assembled with an eye to edifying young minds in "the correctness of taste and refinement of thought."

By mid-century, factories were churning out trifles, furniture and appliances for the burgeoning middle class. Broadsides, mail-order catalogs and trade cards hawked the chic, the useful, the ludicrous. A musical device, tucked in a bustle, played "God Save the Queen" when sat upon. A toy rabbit rose mechanically out of a green cabbage. An electrically powered Health Jolting

The sterling-silver thimble case was made by the Unger brothers in the 1890s. The window shade tassels are from the 1880s. Scattered among the border of trade cards and canning labels are photo-portrait buttons of loved ones, worn as lapel decorations.

chair promised to jolt backpains right out the front parlor door. With the flick of a lever, a child's high chair on rollers converted to a rocker. New-fangled cooking aids—the double boiler, cherry pitter, apple peeler and rotary beater—lightened the load in the kitchen, as did the new washing machine and updated cookstove.

Between 1840 and 1900, women's mass-market magazines emerged as a powerful force in shaping the family mores and domestic life of the new nation. For their own entertainment and edification, mothers subscribed to *Godey's Lady's Book*, *Graham's Magazine* and *Peterson's Ladies' National Magazine*. In long, flowery paragraphs, articles offered practical advice on subjects ranging from "How a Lady Can Make Money and Not Lose Social Caste" (taking in lodgers and painting marine scenes on seashells were two suggestions) to early marriage, long engagements, how to clean sponges and broil rump steaks. For the most part, no topic in the public interest was off limits (with the exception of sex and, in *Godey's*, religion, the Civil War and politics). Lachrymose fiction, poetry, sheet music, ministerial advice, recipes, patterns for knitted, tatted, glued and stitched handmade products, and the all-important, hand-tinted fashion plates filled these self-help bibles.

Other publications

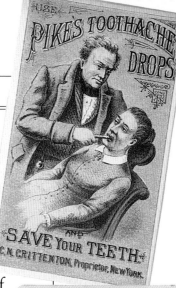

were aimed at a broader—and male—readership: *Frank Leslie's Illustrated Weekly* and *Everybody's Magazine*; *The Atlantic Monthly*, under the direction of well-known editors such as William Dean Howells and James Russell Lowell; *McClure's* with its star muckrakers, Ida Tarbell and Lincoln Stephens. *Harper's Weekly*, which rather grandly billed itself as "A Journal of Civilization," combined the utilitarian with the sensational. Capitalizing on America's desire to be educated, cultured and knowledgeable, these magazines covered politics, current events, fashion, science, gossip, history, travel and entertainment.

Advertisements ran a wide gamut: Columbia Bicycles, Royal Baking Powder, Cures for Opium Addiction, dress suits to hire, office carpets, Mayflower cookstoves, Dr. Scott's Electric Corsets and the Tricora Relief Corset ("I can stoop with such ease"). Ads lauded the efficacy of "Roman, Russian, Turkish and Electric baths for The Relief and Cure of All Nervous Affections, Rheumatism, Dyspepsia and other forms of chronic disease, with careful attention given to cleanliness, comfort and a thorough system of ventilation."

Special-interest magazines filled in niches. Reflecting the growing diversity of an industrializing nation, journals such as *The Dairyman* and *American Whig Review* disappeared from view, replaced by *The American Railroad Journal*, *The Manufacturer and Builder*, *Popular Science Monthly*, *The Phrenology Journal* and *The Art Interchange*, a fancy home-decorating manual.

B elieving that their sons and daughters could rely on a rosy future, and wanting to equip them to derive its maximum benefits, Victorian parents subscribed to *St. Nicholas* and other children's magazines. A mainstay for two generations, *St. Nicholas* serialized works by some of the nation's foremost writers—among them Louisa May Alcott (*Eight Cousins*), Frances Hodgson Burnett (*Little Lord Fauntleroy*), Mark Twain (*Tom Sawyer*

Children's parties were often as elaborate as the ones their elders gave for themselves. Tea parties for as many as fifty guests were not unusual. After dancing, games and a magic lantern show, children dined at tables set with white linen and silver. Tea, sweet cakes, ices, and fresh fruit in season were served on the family's best china. Maud Humphrey, in gentle pastels, portrays the chubby-cheeked guests.

Illustrator Kate Greenaway dressed her small subjects in Empire gowns and breeches.

MAUD HUMPHREY

———•———

*B*abes of the Year, a lavish picture book of winsome toddlers, was an instant success when published in 1888. It's author was Maud Humphrey, and for the next twenty years her fat-cheeked children would peer with sweet innocence from advertisements, children's books, calendars and greeting cards.

In the 1880s publishers generally preferred women illustrators, believing that they understood children best and had childlike minds themselves. Maud Humphrey certainly did not have a childlike mind, nor was she particularly close to her three children. She was strong-willed and determined—more respected than loved, according to her son, Humphrey Bogart.

Abroad) and Rudyard Kipling ("Rikki Tikki Tavi" from *The Jungle Book*). Such celebrated poets as Henry Wadsworth Longfellow and Robert Louis Stevenson also were commissioned to write verse specifically tailored to its young audience.

In this exploding periodicals market, competition was fierce for both circulation and advertising. Dress patterns and other innovative promotions such as "chromos," the nineteenth-century version of posters, were offered as subscription inducements. Hungry for color and culture, Americans signed up by the thousands. By 1890, there were 3,000 periodicals in print in the United States, and advertisers were spending $360 million to get their message across.

Picking blackberries, dabbling toes in a sleepy brook, playing cat's cradle and rolling hoops, weaving clover necklaces and blowing a wish on a dandelion—such were the pleasures of Victorian childhood. And no one caught the gossamer threads of this innocent world, its simplicities and solemnities, like Kate Greenaway, artist, author, illustrator, fashion designer. Her enchanting poems and wide-eyed children in Empire-style gowns, wide sashes and breeches were the *jeune mode* of two generations.

Reading aloud was a national pastime. Poetry, nonsense rhymes, limericks, mysteries, adventure stories were read to and by old and young alike. Picture books—the senti-

A red-hatted pixie child delivers his sister a poke on one of Maud Humphrey's calendars —a household fixture at the turn of the century.

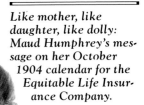

Like mother, like daughter, like dolly: Maud Humphrey's message on her October 1904 calendar for the Equitable Life Insurance Company.

Dewy-eyed and fresh as the meadow flowers that surround them, these bonny children decorated an 1892 calendar (left) and a stovepipe cover (right) used to seal a pipe during the summer.

mental, poignant, dewy-eyed children of artist Maud Humprey, the whimsical, detailed calligraphic illustrations of Walter Crane— were read again and again.

Parents took their children seriously, sparing neither rod nor love. Rules were clear-cut, infractions punished swiftly, but Victorian children were also doted on by an entire world of nannies and nursemaids, a retinue of aunties, cousins and grannies. They were dressed in Lord Fauntleroy velvet breeches and Alice-in-Wonderland pinafores; given elaborate parties; smothered with too many toys; petted, fawned over, adored.

While Victorians passionately espoused education, they were less passionate about paying for it. Teachers had to make do on meager incomes; even governesses were paid a pittance, their annual salary roughly equaling the cost of a mistress's daytime frock.

In the little red school-

Merit cards were awarded for deportment, neatness and diligence all highly valued in Victorian America.

houses that dotted rural America in the 1800s, education was often primitive. Slates, hornbooks and learning by rote were the teacher's tools, and pen and paper if the school district was rich enough to provide them. For rewards, pupils received merits of excellence in punctuality, diligence and deportment—attributes that were highly valued by the new industrial economy.

Schoolhouses were built every six square miles, the distance a child could comfortably walk round-trip in one day. The school year was pegged to farmwork: children got out of school in May for spring planting and did not return until after fall harvest.

School marms came and went with rapidity. Often boarding with a local family, a teacher had little privacy, but sufficiently good visibility to meet a suitor well beyond the six-square-mile range. She was expected to be in good health, neat in dress but not fancy; gentle-mannered and resourceful in the face of discomfort, which could include snowstorms, poison ivy or chilblains.

On sunny days there were picnics, games of hide-and-seek, marbles and skipping rope in the schoolyard, declamation contests and box suppers to raise money. In its small way, the schoolhouse was a minor hub of life for the families who lived within its nesting area.

FULL STEAM AHEAD

PROSPERITY AND OPTIMISM
GO WEST, YOUNG MAN
INVENTIONS AND INGENUITY

In the opening decades of the nineteenth century, America was heady with optimism, excitement, expansion. With the Louisiana Purchase, the new nation had more than doubled in size. The steam engine promised to free men forever from the tedious, backbreaking labor of the industrial revolution. Steamships and steam locomotives would provide cheap transportation to the heartland, where lush prairies, forests, rivers and mountains lay waiting to be explored. Americans were jubilant with the expectation.

By mid-century, after John Marshall's discovery of gold at Sutter Creek in California, the movement west had begun in earnest, and all along the way small-town America bristled with enterprise. The daily unloading of freight at the railway station told it all: threshers, manure spreaders, rolls of barbed wire, boxes of refrigerated lettuce, iced barrels of oysters from Chesapeake Bay, crates of oranges and lemons from the West, bolts of calico, the new Viyella (a cotton-and-wool twill), French ribbons and Belgian lace—products that had never before been seen on the store counters of rural America.

Sometimes passengers in baggy clothes with strange accents wandered off the train, lugging their lumpy parcels and strange ideas along Main Street, in search of jobs and excitement. Tradesmen, shopkeepers and traveling salesmen zealously "drummed" the nation's products to these newcomers, eager to look American as quickly as possible.

By the time the overland transcontinental railroad was completed in 1869, Leland Stanford, Charles Crocker, Collis Huntington and Mark Hopkins had cornered more than the supply route to the Nevada territory. They had millions, political power, and fame.

Prosperity led to leisure activities and the celebration of new riches. For rural America, the county fair was a summertime culmination of labor. Fruits, vegetables, livestock, quilts, cakes and pies, and farm skills were proudly, if competitively, displayed. For the wealthy, the beach club, golf club, yacht club and tennis casino were the center of recreation and relaxation.

Making money became the new American birthright, and invention was one way of acquiring it. In their number and scope, the inventions of the nineteenth century were simply staggering. In 1816, three thousand patents were issued in the United States; by 1896, the figure would rise to fifty-six thousand. The telephone, telegraph, typewriter, Edison's talking machine, Henry Ford's Model T—all were invented between 1860 and 1909. Isaac Singer developed the lockstitch sewing machine. George Otis, a master mechanic at a bedstead factory, perfected a safety mechanism for a hoist that made the elevator possible. John Hyatt invented celluloid, used in making such Victorian necessities as billiard balls, shirt collars and fake ivory jewelry. John Roebling developed steel cable strong enough to build bridges, then used it in the construction of the Brooklyn Bridge. When barbed wire was invented in 1874, western cattle ranges began to be fenced and the

By the 1840s, the lurching, bone-shaking stagecoach was a thing of the past. Locally owned, short-haul rail lines were linking towns of the Northeast. In the large cities, horse-drawn trolleys and steam trams were delivering passengers to their jobs in factories, sweatshops, mills and offices with relative comfort and relative punctuality; the latter was a highly valued attribute in the new industrial America.

Unlike the hot-air balloons of wealthy sporting enthusiasts, Count Zeppelin's cigar-shaped dirigible could actually be steered by a pilot. Fascinated, investors immediately began to toy with the possibility of using these huge, lighter-than-air ships for transatlantic freight and passenger service.

American cowboy passed into legend.

Everybody believed he could build a better mousetrap, and a lot of people did. Nobody said no. Nobody waited for a doctoral degree, a government grant or corporate research dollars. In obscure backyard sheds, in basement laboratories and corner garages, hometown inventors—most of them young, many without formal education—tinkered and fiddled and discussed all the way down to the general store.

Young Cyrus McCormick watched his father, a farmer and blacksmith in Virginia's back country, struggle to invent a mechanical reaper. When the father

MARKETING COMES OF AGE

With such a ravishing array of goods arriving by rail, new merchandising methods were needed. Dry-goods stores mushroomed into labyrinths of basement and loft spaces, and by mid-century three merchandising geniuses—Marshall Field, John Wanamaker and A.T. Stewart—had built marble-and-gilt emporiums of fashion in Chicago, Philadelphia and New York. Promised "fair, equal and elegant treatment," customers of all classes flocked to look as much as buy, sitting on velveteen settees and sipping claret lemonade as they were waited upon.

In 1872 Montgomery Ward started selling its goods to rural America in a one-page price list; three years later, the list had become a catalog of 152 pages. The Sears, Roebuck catalog followed in 1893. With the advent of rural free delivery in 1896, the mail-order business boomed.

gave up, Cyrus took over and by 1834 had patented the reaper that would make America the world's premier wheat producer and himself a millionaire.

Orville and Wilbur Wright, two bachelor brothers who owned a bicycle shop in Dayton, Ohio, became obsessed with the idea of manned flight. Every November, when the bicycle business slowed down, the brothers went to Kitty Hawk, North Carolina (where, according to the U.S. Weather Bureau, the steadiest and most consistent winds along the Eastern seaboard could be found), and struggled to perfect their flying machine under their mother's proviso: Be home by Christmas. On December 9, 1903, Orville stayed aloft in the first manned, heavier-than-air ship for ten seconds. The

Although the notion of a transcontinental railroad had floundered around California for decades, it was Theodore Judah who finally brought it to fruition. Having obtained the seed money, he mapped the route and persuaded an edgy, wartime Congress to put up millions. Yet his name was never mentioned when the final Golden Spike was driven in 1869 at Promontory Point in Utah.

brothers, in their early thirties, had launched the space age—and managed to be home for the holidays.

Labeled "addled" by his schoolteacher, six-year-old Thomas Edison left school for good and thereafter learned his lessons at home from his mother. By the time he was nine, the restless young Edison was testing physics theories in his basement laboratory. By the time he was seventy-five, he had patented, alone and with others, a thousand inventions—among them, the phonograph, the incandescent light bulb and the movie camera.

George Pullman left school at fourteen and became a cabinetmaker in upstate New York. When he patented cherrywood railway car seating that converted into a bed, he ushered in a new era of luxury travel and made a fortune in the process.

Only when steamers began plying the great rivers of America in the mid-1800s did immigrants find a cheap, viable transportation route to the prairie lands of the Midwest. On the Ohio, Mississippi and Missouri rivers, steamboats carried settlers, tools, equipment and supplies inland and raw materials and agricultural products—wool, wheat, corn, whiskey, hogs and cattle—to seaport markets.

To celebrate the world's cornucopia of industrial riches, world trade fairs came into vogue. Prince Albert, who believed industrial products would be the moral and material salvation of the world and eliminate wars, badgered London's Great Exhibition into existence in 1851 over the objections of Parliament. Housed in the Crystal Palace, under a sixty-four-foot-high glass dome designed by Joseph Paxton, the exhibition was a glorious hodgepodge of the frivolous, the ornamental, and serious industrial inventions. One British journalist described a "wonderful new material, indiarubber, for which innumerable uses were being found. . . . We already find the Goodyear Company in the field. Another farsighted gentleman was A. Asher of New Orleans, who has sent a machine for manufacturing ice through the agency of sulphuric acid. Samuel Colt presented the first revolver . . . in which the chamber and not the barrels revolved, an exhibition which caused a sensation among the military." Ten

STEAM TAKES OVER

In the early 1800s, men had begun to experiment with steamboats. Timorous at first, they equipped them with auxiliary sails, just in case the steam engines failed. By 1838 the "just in case" sails were abandoned, and in its historic voyage *The Great Western* crossed the Atlantic from England to New York in 15 days under steam alone. Encouraged by this success, the Cunard Steamship Line began to weave a monolithic network of oceanic trade routes connecting the British colonial ports of Alexandria, Bombay, Madras, Calcutta, Sydney, Melbourne, and Canberra.

Under the Crystal Palace's twenty-five acres of glass, twenty-nine nations displayed their wares. The Queen of Spain sent her crown jewels; France, champagne made from rhubarb; England, a model of the Suez Canal (which was not built until eighteen years later) and a silent alarm clock that woke the sleeper by turning the bed over.

The Eiffel Tower, soaring 984 feet above the Paris Exposition, exemplified the stunning technological triumphs of the Victorian era. Oblivious to danger, engineers had proceeded in the profound belief that no height was beyond their reach. In the 1880s, improvements in structural steel enabled Alexandre Gustave Eiffel to design the skeleton of the Statue of Liberty and Chicago engineers to erect the Home Insurance Building, forerunner of the American skyscraper.

years later, during the Civil War, that "sensation" made Samuel Colt a wealthy man.

When the Crystal Palace closed after thirteen months, the Great Exhibition had broken all attendance projections and handsomely repaid investors. Queen Victoria declared herself "quite beaten" with the beauty and vastness of it all.

It was the sheer grandeur of machines—power lathes, pumps, drills, a hydraulic ram, presses, textile looms—that dominated Philadelphia's Centennial Exposition twenty-five years later. Young Thomas Edison sent his "multiplex" telegraph, which could send several simultaneous messages over one wire. Alexander Graham Bell exhibited a "speaking tube" that could project the human voice hundreds of miles. But it was the thirty-foot-high Corliss Double Walking-Beam Steam Engine that stole the show. On opening day of the exposition, Chauncey de Pew, a New York senator, declared: "This day belongs not to America, but to the World.... We celebrate the emancipation of man."

Steam, Victorians believed, *was* the emancipation of man. The mournful whistle of a steamboat or steam locomotive fired men's souls, opening new horizons. Steamships poked into far-flung corners of the world, transhipping their exotic new products onto railroads that reached the small towns of America for one-tenth the cost of freight wagons traveling on poor, back-country roads.

By the 1840s, steamboats were churning along the nation's great rivers: the Hudson, Mississippi and Ohio. Coastal steamers carried passengers in elegant staterooms between Maine, Boston, Newport, New York, Philadelphia, Savannah, New Orleans. From Maine, prefabricated Greek Revival housing parts—columns, lintels, door frames—were shipped to Mississippi delta plantations. On the return journey up the coast, ships picked up tobacco, rice and cotton for New England's textile mills. From Down East seaports, smelly little menhaden fish were pulverized and shipped south to fertilize cotton fields.

The Cunard Steamship Line, founded in 1840, was sending ships outward bound from England with manufactured goods and returning with raw materials from the British colonies: cotton, wool, silks and furs; ivory and precious minerals; coffee, rice, beef and mutton. In the 1830s, the U.S. government ordered its foreign diplomats to send home botanical specimens that might prove to be of commercial or medicinal value. The Americans who could not book romantic passages to romantic places could at least buy romantic products: cashmere shawls, paisley

BETTER MOUSETRAPS

1846. Anesthesia successfully demonstrated before an audience of New England surgeons

1851. The first perambulator, a three-wheeled baby carriage made of lightweight birchwood, shown at London's Great Exhibition

1857. Installation of the first passenger elevator, in a New York department store

1863. Inauguration of the Philadelphia steam tram

1863. Paper dress patterns patented by Ebenezer Butterick

1873. Installation of San Francisco cable cars

1874. Refrigerated beef first shipped east by Philip D. Armour

1876. Introduction of Charles Scholes' prototype commercial typewriter at the Philadelphia Centennial Exposition, enabling women for the first time to enter the sanctuary of corporate America; unveiling of Alexander Graham Bell's telephone at the Philadelphia Centennial Exposition

SURF BEAUTIES

It was the independent, "go-ahead" sports-minded American woman who led the way to greater freedom in bathing apparel. In the 1880s, at the beaches near Baltimore, women were first reported as appearing without stockings. After bare skin, what on earth could be next? The answer was knickerbockers, worn for bicycling. By the end of the century, American heiresses were giving "come as you are" parties called sans façons. Such casualness marked the beginning of the end of Victorian women's enslavement to stays and bustles.

silks, Indian brass, willow-pattern porcelains, spices, ivory, teak furniture and silky long-stapled cottons—luxuries that simply would have been unobtainable without the cheap freight rates made possible by steam.

"Steam," wrote Sarah Hale, editor of *Godey's Lady's Book*, "will annihilate space and time." And by the 1840s railroads *had* virtually eliminated distances between New England villages and crossed the rocky gorges of upstate New York. The New York, New Haven and Hartford and the Boston and Maine had spanned the impossible: hundreds of rocky inlets puncturing the New England coast from New York to Maine.

Railroad fever rose to its highest pitch when the Golden Spike was driven at Promontory Point, Utah, in 1869, connecting the Atlantic and Pacific coasts. Engineer Theodore Judah's *tour de force*, a railroad crossing the Sierras, was his dream come true. Church bells pealed across the nation. In village squares, cannons thundered a salute to one nation indivisible.

Rail lines west of the Mississippi grew from 3,000 miles of track in 1865 to 72,000 in 1890. On the Delaware-Lackawanna, a darling angel in white named Phoebe Snow completed a day's journey without so much as a speck of soot on her pearly gown. Her virginal white journey proclaimed the superiority of the D & L's

A proper Victorian father was responsible for providing a healthful environment for his family, and seaside summer holidays became the leitmotif. *Harper's New Monthly archly declared in November 1878 that New Yorkers in summer headed out of town and that the narrow tract from Thirty-fourth Street to Fifty-ninth Street, between Fourth Avenue and Sixth, became "a brownstone Sahara."*

anthracite coal over dirty bituminous burned by competitors. So successful was her promotional trip that the Delaware-Lackawanna to this day is called the Route of Phoebe Snow.

Plush hotels grew up as railroads reached into the lush American countryside. At Saratoga Springs, rich, fashionable bachelors from Boston, New York and Philadelphia mingled with belles from Savannah, Atlanta and New Orleans, many of them arriving by private railroad car on the Delaware Hudson Line, which ran from New York City to Montreal. The Florida Central served the Ponce de León, Henry Flagler's terra cotta Spanish Renaissance sand castle in St. Augustine. The Chesapeake and Ohio passed the porticoed White Sulphur Springs Hotel in West Virginia and connected with the stuffy and staid Homestead in Hot Springs, Virginia, where Southern belles sought beaux along with the pine-scented mountain breezes. One such belle was Irene Langhorne, of the FFV Langhornes (FFV meaning First Family of Virginia), who arrived at The Homestead each summer with her family to take up residence on Virginia Row, bringing, among other things, a pair of goats and a goat cart. "I loved it, I loved it, I loved it," Irene recalled years later. "I never wore a speck of makeup of any kind—not even powder and I ate everything. Big breakfasts, big dinners and big suppers. Hot breads and beaten biscuits, too." Despite such indulgence, the

When I was down beside
   the sea
A wooden spade they gave
   to me
To dig the sandy shore.
My holes were empty like a
   cup,
In every hole the sea came up,
Till it could come no more...
—From "At the Seaside," in
   A Child's Garden of Verses
   by Robert Louis Stevenson

In 1869 Empress Eugénie of France, aboard the royal yacht Aigle, opened the Suez Canal with a flotilla of boats, trumpets and fanfare. For engineer Ferdinand de Lesseps the fifty-mile cut was a tour de force, halving the nautical miles between Europe and India.

eighteen-year-old Irene kept her twenty-two-inch waist, married Charles Dana Gibson and became the model for the popular Gibson Girl.

Railroads, the great equalizer, also brought the good life within the reach of Everyman. Newly completed subways and elevateds in New York, Boston and Chicago generated the nation's newest real estate boom: the suburbs, where the middle class could build their rural-style Gothic cottages. Interurbans connected the towns of the northeast corridor and ran along the industrial crescent of Lake Erie, providing working-class families with a way to get to the country. At the end of the line, they could picnic in a shady grove, cruise on a river steamer, sunbathe at the beach, take a dip in the sea, or spend a vacation—a new concept of industrialized, middle-class America.

Amusement parks and honky-tonk boarding house communities grew up along the main rail lines. Outside Boston was Revere Beach. For New Yorkers, there was Coney Island, Rye Playland and the Rockaways. In New Jersey, the Seacoast Railway had transformed a mile-wide strip of beach that ran for 100 miles between Sandy Hook and Cape May to an endless chain of hotels and boarding house resorts. By 1893, Atlantic City alone had 400 wooden

DARWIN'S CHALLENGE

The Victorian sense of order was severely shaken by *The Origin of Species*, published in 1859 by English naturalist Charles Darwin and based on observations during a world-wide voyage of the H.M.S. *Beagle*. Darwin's theory, that human life has evolved by genetic adaption through the millennia, i.e., survival of the fittest—quite simply knocked the biblical story of creation into a cocked hat.

Darwin, a prudent, gentle man, was fully aware of the conflict his theory would cause between religion and science— a conflict he archly called "a simple muddle." If indeed the order of life was not divine, how then could Victorians justify their free-wheeling business tactics, their *carte blanche* to expropriate, to acquire and spend? Darwin, who refused to defend his theory, retired into semireclusivity, protected from the raging controversy by his beloved wife.

hotels with a capacity for 50,000 guests; boarding houses accommodated another 30,000, and private cottages, 20,000. A British visitor to Atlantic City reported that after a five-course breakfast, he could read the Philadelphia and New York morning papers, sit in his wicker chair on the veranda watching "pretty girls in airy, almost angelic nothings," stroll the boardwalk or take a plunge in the surf. Most curious, he found, was the American male's passion for gunning. At the far end of the beach men would ensconce themselves in beach chairs and fire away at little birds called sand snipes, "so swift of foot and wing that one brace will furnish sport for a whole day."

As Americans of all classes fled cities for the tonic of the sea, Satan and his servant, Sin, were sure to follow. Vacationers with fat purses in holiday moods were seduced by gambling and its twin devil, liquor. The more pious, seeking "the Pearl of Great Price" (a nineteenth-century euphemism for the salvation of one's soul), established religious camp meeting grounds, off limits to such evils. Believers at first clustered their tents around the great tabernacles of hymn and prayer, but ultimately replaced them with tiny, fairy-tale gingerbread cottages. Many of these Victorian communities exist today, among them Ocean Grove in New Jersey, Oak Bluffs on Martha's Vineyard, Chautauqua and Shelter Island in New York.

In the 1890s, bicycle mania gripped both sides of the Atlantic. The safety bicycle, a chain-driven two-wheeler with pneumatic tires, had made its début in London in 1885, and now all social classes rode forth on the teetering symbol of freedom. For the shopgirls and factory workers, who rarely traveled beyond the end of the trolley line, the bicycle meant adventure. Young bucks and their bicycle leagues raced back-country roads. Middle-aged matrons took lessons behind the barn. And their daughters wheeled away in daring, divided skirts. Unwittingly or not, their outfits labeled them as members of the nation's newest political class, the New Woman.

Not everyone was overjoyed with the new bicycle freedom. One bride-to-be complained bitterly in *Godey's Lady's Book* in 1893: "Can you imagine the heartache of a newly-engaged girl who fears she has a rival for the affections of her husband-to-be

In 1896, the Buffum Manufacturing Company of Abington, Massachusetts, produced an eight-cylinder, 100-horsepower racing automobile that weighed 2,600 pounds and skimmed six inches above the ground.

...a bicycle? I must say that I was fascinated with the manly, handsome figure and just loved that bicycle until I heard nothing for days but machine, machine, machine!...Today, one of the loveliest of the season, inviting all abroad by its perfectness, finds me here in my room, a disappointed unhappy girl! It's no use. I can't stand it. If he wants his bicycle *all* the time, he can't have me. I'm miserable and lonely and don't want to get married."

Smaller in scale, but no less important to progress than the train and steamship, was the steam-powered carriage that first appeared in Paris in the eighteenth century. By the 1830s, English steam coaches with wheels ten feet in diameter were running at a clip of seventeen miles per hour. By the 1860s, costly, light carriages for two were steaming through the streets at twenty miles per hour. Intensely disliked for their noise and for affrighting the dray horses of the working class, these frivolous early contraptions engendered such a public outcry that they were remanded to obscurity.

In 1863 Belgian engineer J.J. Étienne Lenoir built the first true motor car on three wheels (his first customer was Alexander II, Tsar of Russia), and thirty years later Karl Benz of Germany introduced a four-wheeled gas-driven model called the Victoria. The twin Stanley brothers, Francis and Freelan, experimented with steam and in 1897 came up with the Stanley Steamer, which logged an unprecedented speed of 127 miles an hour.

"Military experts have long agreed that the bicycle will play an important part in the next war. France is already considering the matter. Under the command of Captain Gerard, a French army officer, a battalion of cyclist soldiers has been assiduously practising feats which are usually performed by cavalry....On the regular safety bicycle, a rapid-firing gun is fixed between the handles....It is easy to perceive that charges made by a couple of hundred men riding abreast...would be more deadly than a charge of twice that number of cavalry."

—Reprinted in the Paris edition of the New York *Herald*, December 13, 1886, from the London *Daily Mail*

In the first decade of the twentieth century, the automobile (variously called a motor fly, mocole, motor rig, autobaine and auto-kinetic) remained a toy of the rich until Henry Ford put his cheap, four-cylinder Model T on the market in 1909. Ford's genius lay in converting the automobile from a plaything of the rich to a necessity for the middle class. He mass-produced his cars on an assembly line, making his apocryphal remark that buyers could have any color car they wanted as long as it was black. A superb salesman, he settled on a very simple formula: increase volume and reduce price, a cycle he repeated over and over again. From its initial cost of $950, the open touring model's price dropped to

$690 in 1911, then to $550 in 1913. In 1913, total U.S. automobile sales rose to 461,500 cars. Most of them were Model Ts.

Ford also recognized the importance of service to his buyers, who were after all just graduating from the horse and buggy. A horse, for all its cantankerous ways, was at least a known entity.

In the first decade of the new century, America was moving full steam ahead into an era of progress from which there was no turning back.

THE BIG WHEELS

Henry Ford, Charles Goodyear (vulcanized rubber), Andrew Carnegie (steel) and John D. Rockefeller (Standard Oil) were the industrial titans who made the American automotive industry the envy of the world. Not until the mid-twentieth century did Americans begin to discover that what was good for General Motors was not necessarily good for America.

ALONG THE GARDEN PATH

COUNTRY ESTATES AND
COTTAGE GARDENS

HOME-GROWN HORTICULTURE

NATURE'S GRANDEUR

Homemakers quilted roses on coverlets, embroidered them on bureau "tidies," and laid Brussels carpets with cabbage rose patterns on their parlor floors. They made rose-hip jam from the fruit, and rose attar, pressing one hundred full-headed damask roses with petals the size of silver dollars to make one ounce of the rose oil. Rose potpourris in sachet bags were given as bon voyage gifts to conceal the foul smells of journey by rail.

"How much happiness, how much pure pleasure....verdant lawns and smiling flowers all breathe forth to us, in true, earnest tones, a domestic feeling that at once purifies the heart and binds us more closely to our fellow beings!"
—Andrew Jackson Downing in Cottage Residences, *1842*

So passionate were the Victorians in their romance with nature that they poured their hearts, their souls and their pocketbooks into gardens and flowers, windowboxes and ferneries, lawns for croquet, tennis and badminton. They moved their parlors to the outdoors, erecting gazebos and grape arbors equipped with rustic twig chairs and cast-iron furniture. They planted impractical expanses of lawn and built carriage roads with picturesque vistas and romantic glades at great expense; hired armies of gardeners to maintain intricate flower beds, called "carpet bedding," that required three plantings each season to remain fresh and sparkling.

Many considerations, historical, nostalgic and spiritual, braid into the Victorian love of gardens. Most everyone in nineteenth-century

Victorians adored roses above all. They gathered voluptuous bouquets of cabbage roses in delicate hues of ivory, pale lemon, apricot and blush pink; planted Pompeian red climbers that cascaded over arbors all summer long; mounted fiery orange grandifloras in Viennese glass épergnes in their front hallways.

America was on the move: westward to greener pastures, cityward to make a fortune, upward on the social ladder. Immigrants were on the move to jobs anywhere. But they all sought a dream in common: a plot of land. For some, this meant food, abundance and security; for others, the comfort of a garden like the one back home. But for most, gardens were a reward and a fantasy—an Eden of fruited elegancies, leafy bowers and romantic niches. Such a place of delight demonstrated to the world that Providence had indeed seen fit to reward the owner for his thrift, industry and diligence.

And finally Victorians sought spiritual renewal in larger gardens, contemplating immortality, the sublimity of nature, and the Almighty who had so ably assisted His flock in conquering the brooding forces of American frontiers. They landscaped rural cemeteries; built great urban parks in Boston, New York and Brooklyn; founded aboretums and horticultural societies. Everyone celebrated nature in his own way.

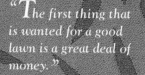

"The first thing that is wanted for a good lawn is a great deal of money."
—Dr. Trimble of the American Institute, 1861

Philadelphians founded the Pennsylvania Horticultural Society in 1829; societies in New York, Cincinnati and Boston followed. Members were ardent plant propagators: they experimented with new fruit and vegetable hybrids, swapped root stocks and seedlings, competed fiercely for blue ribbons at annual exhibitions.

The societies sponsored rural cemeteries, prudently planting one specimen of every kind of tree that could withstand the winter climates. Spaced well apart from one another, each tree today stands full-grown in stately isolation, its texture and shape etched with draftsman's precision against an open sweep of sky.

Although women did not attend funerals, they de-

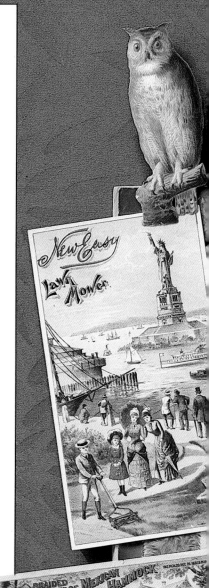

Victorian America, a land "of small pianos and big choruses," liked nothing better than belting out a good hymn—at summer camp meetings, political rallies, community gatherings and churches. Hymns, crossing all denominational lines, celebrated patriotism, God, nature, life everlasting, cherubim and seraphim.

All things bright and
  beautiful
All creatures great and small,
All things wise and wonderful,
The Lord God made them all.

Each little flower that opens,
Each little bird that sings,
He made their glowing colors,
He made their tiny wings...

The purple headed mountain,
The river running by,
The sunset and the morning,
That brightens up the sky;

The cold wind in the winter,
The pleasant summer sun,
The ripe fruits in the garden,
He made them every one...
—Children's hymn by Cecil
Frances Alexander

The sublimity of nature and the awesomeness of God's natural world were cornerstones in the spiritual lives of Victorians. Hardly was there a family, rich or poor, who did not bow to the summons of the Reaper, the Victorian euphemism for death. In His infinite wisdom God gave and God took away, and it was not for the Earthly to ask why. So solace was gleaned from pearly visions of the Hereafter, an angel-ringed firmament free from pain where Loved Ones were rejoined and Little Ones were imagined as spiritual cherubs of myth and beauty.

Trust in the LORD.

Keep thy HEART
with all DILIGENCE;
FOR OUT OF IT
ARE THE ISSUES OF LIFE.

signed and tended the graveside gardens, planting them to look like miniature grottoes. Of a Sunday, family members would gather at the burial plot to commune with the departed and ponder their own mortality. Mourners sat on tiny cast-iron chairs, built to three-quarter scale in order to accommodate all at the gravesite.

Brooklyn's Green-Wood Cemetery, begun in 1838, was such a sylvan retreat. On a spring weekend in the 1850s, ten thousand city dwellers would flock to its flower-spangled hills, a model carefully studied by Frederick Law Olmsted, who was mapping out Central Park.

Andrew Jackson Downing, founder and editor of the influential and much-read *Horticulturist*, advocated miniature versions of the English pleasure garden for the Gothic suburban cottages so fashionable with a burgeoning middle class. Fruit trees, a patch of grass, flowers interwoven with boxwood, a kitchen garden tastefully concealed behind trellised vines—these could be managed, according to Downing, by families on the smallest of incomes, provided the womenfolk would spend an hour or two in the cool mornings tying plants to stakes, picking spent blossoms and weeding. As a spiritual bonus, their hearts would be purified by such salubrious activity.

Like Downing, the owners of the great estates along the Hudson, Ohio, Mississippi and Delaware rivers were passionate horticulturists. They bred new strains of livestock and experimented with vineyards and miniature orchards of citrus and camellia trees in heated "forcing houses."

In hopes of making a fortune in silk, Philadelphian Nicholas Biddle purchased seven thousand mulberry trees of the *Morus multicaulis* variety, an alleged easy-to-grow favorite of silkworms. The trees proved to be a hoax, but Biddle, undaunted, went on to build an elaborate glass-enclosed grapery. There he produced fine grapes from European stock for the dinner tables of Philadelphia.

With the advent of commercial food-processing, the kitchen garden gradually shifted from being an essential source of vegetables and herbs for the family, to a more decorative, nostalgic recreational activity. The more frivolous cultivation of flowers, at last, earned ministerial blessing. Flower growing was declared to be a wholesome, refined and tasteful activity.

By the 1870s, the colorful chromolithographic illustrations on seed packets and in nursery catalogs had made purchasing new plants so irresistible that Reverend Henry Ward Beecher began to inveigh against extravagant expenditures on fashionable new fruits and vegetables. Writing for Downing in the *Horticulturist*, Beecher

AMERICA'S LANDSCAPER

Andrew Jackson Downing, premier park and garden architect, advocated informal landscapes of curving paths, irregular groupings of trees, a Temple of Love buried in verdure to surprise the viewer.

In 1841 he wrote *A Treatise on the Theory and Practise of Landscape Gardening*, and the following year published his influential *Cottage Residences*. In 1846 he founded the *Horticulturist*.

Downing died while planning a 160-acre park in Washington, D.C., with architect Calvert Vaux. In July 1852, the Hudson River steamboat on which he was traveling caught fire. Downing drowned while attempting to rescue fellow passengers. He was thirty-seven years old.

Strange as it seems in twentieth-century America, Victorians in England took fairies quite seriously. Surrounded as they were by ugly smokestacks in soot-laden towns and children begrimed with coal dust, the English wanted to believe in fairies. They illustrated manuscripts and theatrical stage settings with tiny mythical creatures and commissioned paintings of fairies personifying the ideal and the romantic.

PATRONS OF HUSBANDRY

By the 1850s America had pushed her frontiers across the Sierras, and the "plow that broke the plains" was furrowing the rich sod of the Midwest. In 1867 the American Grange was founded, dedicated to the improvement of farming techniques and the agrarian ideals of honesty, patriotism, frugality and industry. America was proud of her farms and farmers, and by 1870 the nation was the world's leading exporter of wheat.

After the Shakers in Pennsylvania introduced seed packaging in the early 1800s, commercial seedsmen began mailing out hand-tinted catalogs. When chromolithography burst its lavish colors on seed boxes and catalogs, the newest and exotic hybrids proved irresistible.

PUMPKIN

WATER MELON
DIXIE.

CABBAGE

PEAS

TILLER

GIANT HIMALAYA BERRY

BURPEE'S
SUNSHINE
POLE BEAN

MUSK MELON EARLY GEM

NEWEST AND BEST

VICK'S EARLY SCARLET GLOBE RADISH.

Compliments of
HOLDEN & ROBINSON.

PARKER & WOOD
SEEDS AND TOOLS
BOSTON.

JAMES VICK, Seedsman,

ROCHESTER,

N. Y.

Cast-iron foundries mass-produced furniture for pergolas, arbors and gazebos (a charming shortened version for "gaze-about") in patterns of twining tendrils, acanthus leaves and ferns that extended the "natural look" of gardens. Statues of deer, lions and weeping maidens were also designed for outdoors, as were fountain sea nymphs holding dolphins aloft.

warned that exotic hybrids, made to look succulent in print, were fussy to grow, likely to wither, and sure to strip a man of his money. Instead the Reverend, himself a modest horticulturist, advised "busy mothers, the laborious middle class and the industrious poor" to stick to such old reliables as wisteria, ivy and clematis.

His advice fell on deaf ears. Plant mania continued unabated. Nurseryman Robert Manning of Salem, Massachusetts, offered one thousand varieties of pear trees for sale. When Thomas Drummond brought back strains of fuchsia and phlox from Texas, and botanist Robert Fortune introduced forsythia and bleeding heart from China, Victorians paid dearly and happily to plant them in their gardens.

Victorian wives decorated their homes with floral handcrafts in every conceivable medium. They hooked cornucopian designs into rugs; made wreaths from dried flowers, human hair, seed pods and pine cones; constructed "moss" paintings by gathering and pasting moss on prenumbered picture grids; crocheted daisy-lace antimacassars, and pinned posies on their bosoms. Ladies of all ages plucked daisy petals to see who loved them and who did not. They painted roses, lilacs and daisies on lamp shades, sugared violets and forget-me-nots for use as cake decorations, and dipped flowers in paraffin to preserve them. Mothers made hollyhock dolls for their daughters, heaped flowers, real and *faux*, onto their hats and, of course, grew them in their gardens.

A suitable occupation for Victorian homemakers of all classes was tending the conservatory, an indoor greenery of ferns, rubber plants, miniature lemon and lime trees, and such exotic scented flowers as jasmine and orange blossoms. Ferneries (even a large bay window would do) became popular, especially after Catherine Beecher assured readers that plants, once indoors, would not give off any poisonous odors.

The Victorian home-garden-

Japanese Hand-Screen.

GOD BLESS

No church supper, ice-cream social or family reunion left a woman without her "busy" work—embroidering flowers onto perforated cardboard wall hangings, pipe holders, covered brick door-stops, bags for holding hair combings, "tidies" for bureau and desk tops.

ing bible, *The Floral Cabinet*, advised that for decorating mirrors, frames and windows, brocades and lace could not be compared to the tasteful elegance of wreathing vines, interlacing sprays and graceful tendrils. Much effort was also expended in the fashioning of love messages from flowers, "those bright earth stars, the alphabet of angels," gathered into nosegays—or tussie-mussies, as Victorians called them.

While women stitched and pasted and wrote poems about flowers, newly minted industrial barons, most of them born on a farm, copied the great villa gardens of fifteenth-century Italian merchant princes. They constructed French parterres and English carpet beds alongside their summer mansions in Saratoga Springs, in Newport, in the Berkshires, and along the Brandywine River in the Delaware Valley.

Nobody, it seems, in Victorian America, would be without the uplift of a garden.

PETERSON'S MAGAZINE, January, 1874.—Design for Cushion, &c. and Border.

, WITH SECTIONS.

ented to the Subscribers of "Peterson" as a Christmas Gi

Stripe for Chair,

FASHIONABLE LADIES

OF BUSTLES AND BAUBLES
MANNERS AND MORALS
ON THE TOWN

For the Victorian woman, no effort was too great to expend on assembling the perfect costume for every social occasion. In the 1890s, the gowns described on a single fashion page of the Paris *Herald* reveal an extraordinary array of fabrics: tulle, batiste and sheer linen lawn; satin and silk velvet; finely crinkled piqué; serge twill and silk muslin; a heavy silk lace called *guipure*; surah, a twilled silk from India; moiré taffeta, alpaca, chenille and foulard; *broche*, a pinstripe woven on the warp; *mousselin de soie*, a thin, stiff silk, and a bouclé Cheviot suiting.

Jewelry was set with obscure minerals and gems, bronze and brass alloys entwining zircons, baroque pearls and scarabs. Horn from horse hooves, when melted, molded and dyed, was fashioned into beautiful, lightweight pendants and pins of lustrous black. Hairpieces were frizzed, furled, curled, braided, knotted or poufed, and skewered into place with immense jeweled hatpins. And, to round out her ensemble, a fashionable woman added a parasol, fan, purse and shawl.

Reflecting the social and political changes in the status of women, fashions over the nineteenth century had moved from the simple Empire gowns of the New Republic to the ornate creations of the Gilded Age. In the first quarter-century, enormous mutton-leg sleeves held sway, progressing to fitted sleeves and finally to the bell sleeves whose filmy overlays of mull, lace and netting caused much anguish over how to eat and drink without dragging a sleeve through the gravy or knocking over a wine goblet. Crinolines were replaced by hoop skirts, which in turn were superseded by the bustle. This extraordinary invention, flattened and gathered in the rear, required twenty-five yards of fabric and could weigh up to

A Victorian lady could bathe in the sea, hike, play tennis or drive her own electric—but never without a hat. By the 1880s hats had climbed to new heights, piled with mounds of flowers, fruits, birds and feathers.

By the end of the century, William Morris and the Arts and Crafts movement in England had popularized the Pre-Raphaelite madonna. With curly tresses flowing au naturel, and decidedly softer, more dewey-eyed than her peer on the opposite page, she appeared in paintings, bookplates and magazine illustrations that appealed to the upper classes.

Runners for ice skates and roller-skate wheels were clamped onto high-top boots.

thirty pounds. To spread the weight, Warner Brothers advertised a flexible skirt supporter (120 bones) for $1.25, warranted not to break over the hips.

Amidst the mounting embellishments of *haute couture*, the ever sensible *Godey's Lady's Book* advised simplicity rather than slavish imitation of court fashions that "often concealed some deformity"—a direct slap at Queen Victoria, whose hoops hid the waddling gait of her abnormally short legs. According to *Godey's*, true gentlewomen wore "fresh lace at the throat and wrists, well-cleaned boots, a crisp handkerchief and spotless gloves." Moreover, they need not be restricted by uncomfortable corsets but should follow the lines of their own figures.

Godey's harangue was hopeless. The fashion battle royale remained the hourglass figure, yes or no—the S-curved body and wasp waist, all achievable with steel,

"*Lillian told me in confidence that Mrs. Beauchamp-Peacock has three silk petticoats. How she made this discovery, I know not, but feel deeply envious. Wonder if this is a married woman's lot? Nannie wears flannel next to her skin, I know.*"
—*Maud Tomlinson in her diary, June 1890*

bones and stays. Dr. and Mrs. Strong staunchly maintained that their corsets would "relieve the delicate and vital organs of all injurious pressures." Not possible, argued Madam Yale in the 1901 edition of *How to Attain Health, Beauty and Happiness*. A corset, she maintained, produced "a sickly, sallow complexion; pale thin, compressed lips; soured tempers, lusterless eyes; lassitude, apathy and stupidity." J. Daine of Paris advocated night corsets to mold the sleeping figure and assured his readers that this product had been adopted at "several courts of Europe."

These bonneted ladies in eighteenth-century garb were pasted into collections of historical fashions.

No single event had greater impact upon nineteenth-century fashion in America than Isaac Singer's lock-stitch treadle sewing machine, which made its début in the late 1850s. Now every homemaker could braid, pleat, tuck, puff, shirr, gather or embroider her own *oeuvre*, cutting her

"*We sauntered in our Hats and wore white wash silks & Lillian twirled a parasol. We judged that our hats outdid the others on display. I had piled linen bows atop a basket of cherries on my hat, which both gave me some extra heighth and was calculated to attract attention. Mr. Wilfred Parker invited us both out to tea, on the strength, I feel, of our hats.*"

— *Maud Tomlinson in her diary, July 1888*

sewing time from twenty hours to three. The parlor prattle was intense: Directoire bonnets, Gainsborough hats, *moyenage* bodices, what fabrics were offered in the Montgomery Ward catalog. (The 1897 catalog included twenty-seven pages of fabrics.)

In Newport mansions and Nebraska farmhouses, women poured over patterns, adapting costumes to pocketbook and circumstances. They gossiped about the newest emporiums of fashion: A.T. Stewart's department store in New York and John Wanamaker's in Philadelphia. With the new concepts of assembling a vast array of goods under one roof and charging a fixed price for each item, Mr. Stewart and Mr. Wanamaker became very rich men. Gone was price haggling, sometimes an embarrassment in small towns since the dry-goods merchant was, like as not, a neighbor and fellow church member.

By the 1890s, whether hand-sewn in front parlors, store-bought or couturier-designed, styles were dictated from Paris

HAGAN'S MAGNOLIA BALM FOR THE COMPLEXION

by the clever, arrogant Charles Worth, arbiter of fashion to royalty and aspirants to royalty. In its 1896 Easter issue, the Pa[?] *Herald* noted that hats had shrunk in size because of the popularity of riding in open carriages; capotes, berettas, capelines and toques, made of straw or stiffened lace, were advised for this outdoor activity. Croquet dresses were "of cambric and lawn, plain and figured in the most brilliant and delicate coloring. . . . If a beautiful hand is to be shown, lace mitts are adopted; these are not, however, as great a protection to the hands as the gloves." For lawn tennis, the fashionable new game imported from England, a white taffeta skirt, white taffeta blouse trimmed with lilies of the valley, and small-brimmed white Panama hat were recommended.

Lunging for a tennis ball, ice skating on the pond or clambering down a bluff in long, heavy skirts and flannel petticoats took delicate balance and fortitude. Even standing upright for long periods of time had its perils. One young thing succumbed to the heat at Ascot and had to be carried out in a swathe of skirts and black bombazine, her ostrich-feathered hat all askew. Once Queen Victo-

EXTRACT

NIGHT BLOOMING CEREUS

ROSE

HAIR OIL

N°   Y_{ds}

INDIA LINON

As their menfolk became part of
the American success story, women
were pampered with jewels, imported
silks and cashmeres, boas of feathers and
furs, and fans of ivory and lace—luxuries often
featured on fabric and perfume labels.

CASHMERE

EAU DE LAVANDE

Ladies' Heeled Boots.

This oval portrait of lovers at a maypole dance is a fabric label. Labels often suggested the romantic possibilities that might ensue should a lady wear a dress made of a charming fabric.

For ladies of breeding, sketching, drawing and even maintaining an art studio were encouraged.

ria had led the way to the beach in her bathing machine, a bathhouse contraption which for modesty's sake was rolled down to the edge of the sea, it became acceptable for ladies to "bathe." And that's all they could do, covered as they were from collarbone to anklebone with knickers, tunic and canvas shoes—a cumbersome if not life-threatening outfit.

The inevitable backlash was led, oddly enough, by American women who were sufficiently *au courant*, rich and independent to thumb their noses, however delicate and demure, at many of the stifling fashion conventions of Paris. Corsets would simply not do for turn-of-the-century sports enthusiasts or for the social workers who attended lectures and prowled unsavory neighborhoods, establishing soup kitchens and opening settlement houses. (Two pioneers, Hull House in Chicago and Henry Street Settlement in New York, are still in operation today.) Women adopted serviceable dark skirts, sparkling starched white "waists" and fitted jackets, which in time became the fashionable, *avant-garde* Gibson-girl look.

MODERN KANGAR

S till, for most young girls in both America and England, marriage was the ultimate goal and "prinking out like a peacock" was the norm. Courtship was a deadly serious business. One's girlhood was scarcely long enough to prepare for so exalted an undertaking as marriage. A properly trained young

While Victorian England embraced the notion of the weaker sex reclining on a divan at the slightest provocation, such supine stances were largely rejected by American women, only one generation away from the frontier.

woman learned to sing, to play the piano or guitar, to dance and be conversant about the light literature of the day. In the upper classes, she would also read the racier French novels of Flaubert, de Maupassant and George Sand, along with their English and American counterparts: Louisa May Alcott, the Brontë sisters, Henry James and Edith Warton.

In the upper classes, housekeeping skills added little to the desirability of a prospective bride. She learned on the job. One English Victorian mother sent a daughter off to her new husband, archly declaring that to run her household all she need know was "how to keep the servants in order and buy good sago," an essential ingredient of puddings.

For afternoon canters, a lady wore an English-style riding habit of midnight blue with a small, veiled hat and carried a gold-headed riding crop.

For most American middle-class brides, the scenario was different. Daughters apprenticed in the kitchen, learning from the "hired girl" how to preserve fruits and vegetables. This was a summer-long task, beginning with the first rhubarb harvest in May and ending with the last October crop of green tomatoes, salvaged from frost and made into pickles and marmalades rich with exotic East Indian spices. In her mother's 1880s Victorian cookbook, one daughter wrote the annotation: "Long will I associate strawberries and cherries with Longfellow and Whittier. All through June I hulled strawberries and pitted cherries with my book open beside me at the piece I was to speak on the last day of school."

Mothers instructed their daughters in the art of planning a "company" dinner, which in the summer might include the following: platters of cold boiled tongue, thinly sliced lemon-flavored veal loaf, chicken salad, baked beans; gold, red and purple jellies; radishes and pickles; great puffy, feathery hot rolls, cheeses under a delicate green glass dome on a carved ash platter, floating island with citron preserves; a devil's-food cake, much the rage in midwestern America in the 1880s, grandly positioned on a high glass cake stand on the walnut sideboard. Of course, wines, clarets and port would be brought from Father's wine closet, to which he alone held the key.

From the "hired" hand, an all-purpose

Hand-embroidered wrist bags carried feminine essentials: a lace handkerchief, calling cards, perfume and pin money.

EDWIN C. BURT,
FINE SHOES.

PRESENTED BY
NOLAN BROS.,
736 & 740 Market St.,
SAN FRANCISCO.

MAGIC
RUSTIC TRIMMED

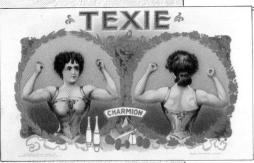

"If the men are the savages, we want her to be their civilizer. We want her to soften their manners, and to teach them all needful lessons of order, society, and meekness, and patience and goodness."
—Mary Melendy, M.D., in Maiden, Wife and Mother, 1901

Pets and birds, in gilded cages and on country terraces, were a favorite subject of calendar art, greeting cards, chromos and posters.

house valet of sorts, a daughter learned how to stretch the big walnut table to its fullest length to accommodate sixteen guests, then polish it with old blankets saturated in lemon wax and wrapped around a brick. The coal-oil lamps in crystal chandeliers had to be trimmed and filled; the parlor carpet turned, the silver scoured, the satin-smooth table linens laid out. And there was the critical, final rite, before the dining room doors were closed in readiness, of determining the seating arrangements that would ensure a steady flow of felicitous conversation. On this, more than anything else, the ultimate success of the dinner depended.

All daughters learned the art of conversation and the even more delicate art of silence. Advised one Dr. Blair in *Godey's* in 1895, "Silence may easily and effectually promote the most useful and elegant conversation without speaking a word. The modes of speech are scarcely more variable than the modes of silence." If, how-

Compliments of Pollard's Dry Goods Corner, West Manchester, New Hampshire.

ever, the silence hung too heavy, *Godey's* never left a damsel in distress: "It is always gratifying to an individual to converse on those topics with which he is most familiar...his calling, profession or favorite pursuits." If those subjects failed to elicit a response, the editors suggested

Enjoy your triumphs, gay
coquette! Your happiness is
brief;
You're like a pretty rose from
which each lover plucks a
leaf.
I pity, though, the husband
who with you his future
mourns;
When all the leaves are
plucked, for him there'll
naught remain but thorns.
—From "Coquette: A
Quatraine," in *Godey's Lady's
Book,* 1881

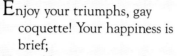

THE *LADY'S* LADY

For three decades, Sarah Hale, editor of *Godey's Lady's Book*, agitated for higher education for women. Early in her crusade, she flattered men into believing that women's education would benefit them. Didn't a husband deserve a stimulating mental companion? Didn't his children deserve the best possible teacher?

Hale upbraided her good friend Matthew Vassar for using the word "female" in the new college he had endowed. "Why degrade the feminine sex to the level of animals?" she asked. He changed the name.

By the end of the century, female seminaries had metamorphosed into four-year institutions. Men's colleges began admitting women, and new colleges for women were being established in many states: Emma Willard in upstate New York, Mt. Holyoke in Massachusetts, Bryn Mawr in Pennsylvania, Randolph Macon Woman's College in Virginia and Sophie Newcomb in New Orleans.

It was only a beginning.

"popular preaching at popular churches and local charities. . . . Schools or benevolent associations are a never-failing source of interest." But, above all, *Godey's* counseled young ladies to "constantly be alert to the signs which an acquaintance sometimes exhibits when desirous of taking his leave."

Concerned about health to the point of hypochondria, Victorians were fastidious. As a courtesy among polite company, those afflicted with colds were expected to wear "respirators" (mouth masks) in public. Women took air baths, disrobing in a room full of fresh air, then scrubbed with a thick, dry towel. *Godey's* advised readers to take weekly baths, to shampoo oily hair twice weekly in the city and once a week in the country. Women collected their own hair combings in small creweled satin bags attached to their dressers; it was more sanitary to use one's own hair in fashioning hairpieces, and, of course, the color match was perfect.

Rest, pure air and contemplation were recommended by Charles Fillmore: "Sit for one half hour every night at nine o'clock and mentally forgive every one against whom you have ill-will or antipathy, even a pet. Mentally ask forgiveness and send it thoughts of love."

With or without such rest and contemplation, the Victorian woman was stepping down from her pedestal to pioneer a radical new role for her sex. Abetted by beauty, artifice and intelligence, she sparked a new era. Women in the twentieth century are still in her debt.

The row of ladies dressed in Marie Antoinette milk-maid costumes (right) is part of a series of historical scrap sheets produced for collections. The art nouveau soap labels (upper right) date from the early 1900s.

HANS WAGNER

MANLY PURSUITS

THE ART OF MAKING MONEY
A GENTLEMAN'S CLUB
THE SPORTING LIFE

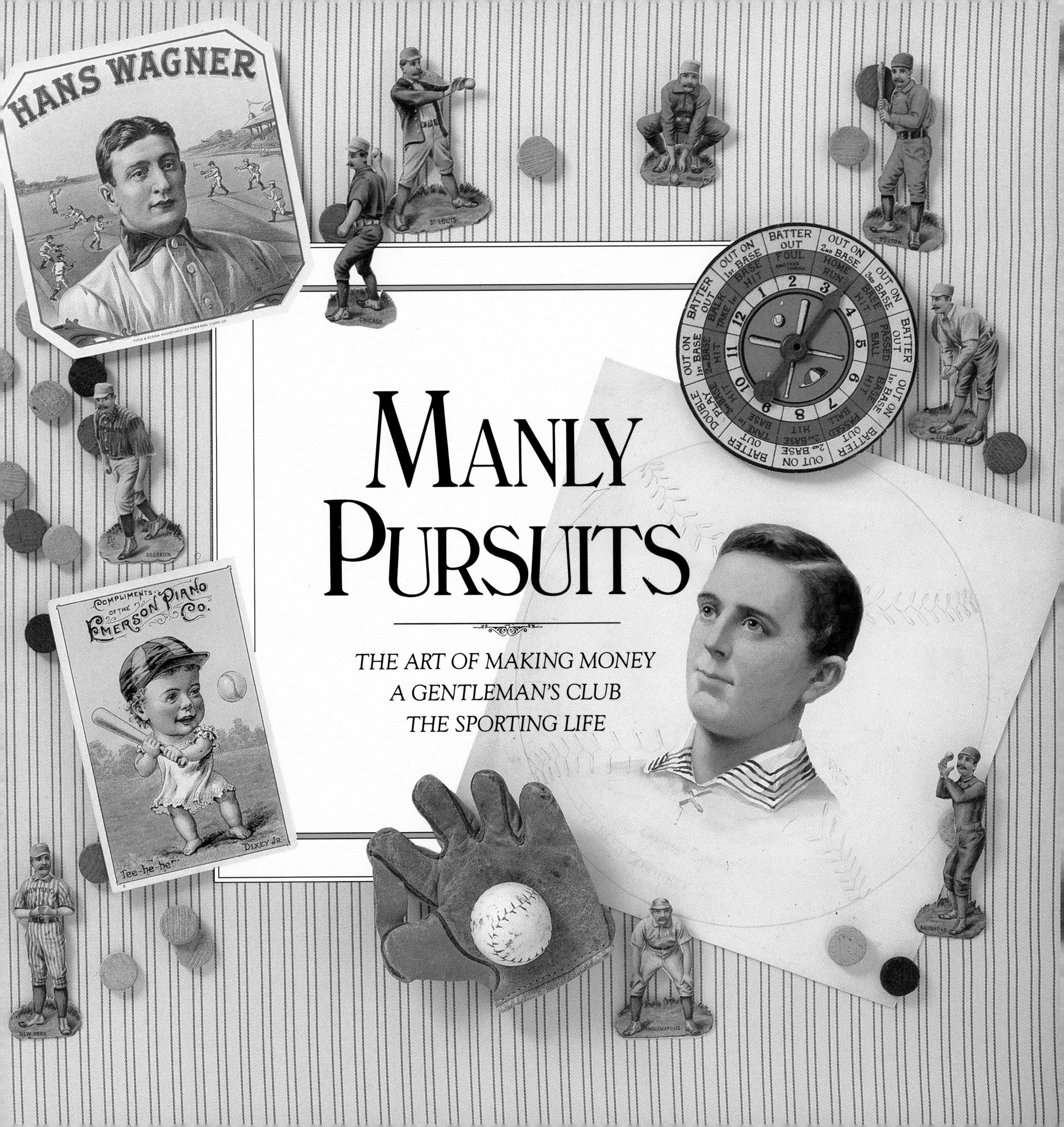

COMPLIMENTS OF THE
EMERSON PIANO CO.

"Tee-he-he"

DIXEY JR

"They are obviously persons of experience—of a somewhat narrow and monotonous experience certainly; an experience of which the diamonds and laces which their wives are exhibiting hard by are, perhaps, the most substantial and beautiful result. . . . They are not the mellow fruit of a society which has walked hand-in-hand with tradition and culture: they are hard nuts, which have grown and ripened as they could. When they talk among themselves, I seem to hear the cracking of the shells."

—Henry James, writing of American men at
Saratoga Springs in The Nation, *summer of 1870*

Although the laissez-faire ethic of Victorian America certainly produced its scalawags, by and large the American entrepreneur took great pride in his work and family, and respected the freedom of opportunity to make money that unleashed the incredible creative energy of the period.

The Victorian man about town was a high-stepping strutter. Pomaded, bejeweled and preened, he paraded the avenue in a derby, frock coat, high stiff collar and silk cravat. With his pearl-handled cane and a fresh flower in his lapel, he was quintessential High Life, spinning the world on his finger. Who ever would guess he was only five years off the farm?

With a passion for display, he dyed his hair, trimmed his goatee and sideburns, waxed and curled the ends of his mustache to stand as big as jib sails, set wing and wing. No amount of fuming by *Godey's Lady's Book* budged the hirsute Victorian gentleman. The bearded face remained in vogue throughout the Gilded Age.

As a man on the move, he fashioned himself to be seen: driving his four-in-hand along the coachways of one of the new urban parks, dining *alfresco* at Delmonico's, strolling under the midnight dazzle of theater marquees on lower Broadway. He immersed himself in the subtler tones of his men's club, enjoying a glass of port, a Havana and gossip: Did Gordon Ben-

In elegant splendor, commuters hurtle along at twenty miles per hour.

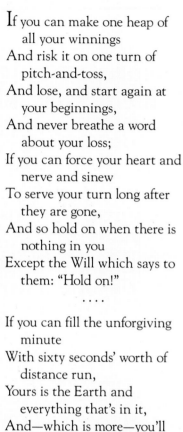

If you can make one heap of
    all your winnings
And risk it on one turn of
    pitch-and-toss,
And lose, and start again at
    your beginnings,
And never breathe a word
    about your loss;
If you can force your heart and
    nerve and sinew
To serve your turn long after
    they are gone,
And so hold on when there is
    nothing in you
Except the Will which says to
    them: "Hold on!"
            . . . .

If you can fill the unforgiving
    minute
With sixty seconds' worth of
    distance run,
Yours is the Earth and
    everything that's in it,
And—which is more—you'll
    be a Man, my son!

    —From "If," by Rudyard Kipling

nett *really* persuade a British army officer to ride his horse into the Newport Reading Room?

But the gossip, the right club and the right clothes were part of a much larger scene—the manly pursuit of making money. Horatio Alger said it all in his dime novels with plots that never varied: a farm boy makes good when he comes to town *if* he sheds his down-home twang, his hayseed manners and baggy knickers, and *if* he keeps his fiscal wits about him. By 1880, 40 percent of agrarian America had done just that. The opportunities were glorious and high sailing, the sounds of prosperity heady with promise: the clatter of dray wagons wrangling their way through crowded streets; the steam whistles of factories, the whang of hammers and shouts of construction crews. Railroads carried consumer goods to small-town America. Tradesmen hustled as they never had before. Everybody was on the move up.

A man could "come into money" by marriage or inheritance, or by his own endeavors—the most respected route, especially if manufacturing was his choice. A man's endeavors had a lot to do with his social class. Patient labor at one's station was one thing, entrepreneurship and diligence another. And diligence in a Yankee was different from diligence in an Englishman. Energy, drive, aggres-

Colorful business cards, left in baskets or trays at the corner store, were collected, traded and pasted into scrapbooks for the beauty and richness of the illustrations.

siveness, persistence, self-reliance, and a directness that would have been unthinkable in an Englishman—these were the American's stock in trade.

Following a trip to England, Henry Ward Beecher, minister to one of the wealthiest parishes in America, observed: "As to business, I found in London that you may go down at nine o'clock to see a man and there is nobody in his office; at ten o'clock the clerks are there; at eleven o'clock some persons do begin to appear. By that time the Yankee has got through half his day." What Beecher did not say was that an Englishman was probably breakfasting at his club. Old Boy ties were vital; schoolboy friendships, deep and enduring; family connections, everything. Connections in America were important, too, but here even casual street connections were cemented by a handshake.

Russell Conwell, Baptist minister, crisscrossed the country giving his famous "Acres of Diamonds" speech, which he also printed and sold as a brochure. His message: "To make money honestly is to preach the gospel." But making money required a certain dispassionate view toward one's fellow man. Immigrants and youngsters were willing to work ten-hour shifts for pennies a day. After dynamiting the slopes of the Sierra Nevada and laying the railroad tracks of the Central Pacific, the Chinese gladly shipped east as strikebreakers.

SOUTHERN AUTOMATION

When James Bonsack of Virginia perfected a machine that could roll 200 cigarettes an hour, cigar smoking was doomed. He teamed up with Buck Duke of Durham, North Carolina, and by 1889 they were producing half of the 2.1 billion cigarettes smoked by Americans each year.

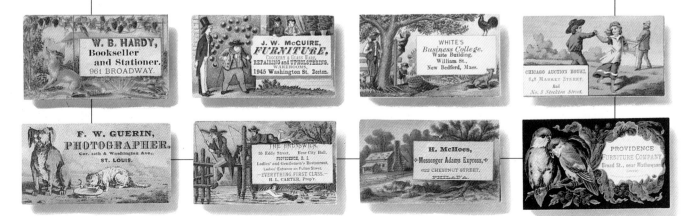

By the time the National Grange of the Patrons of Husbandry was founded in 1867, agrarian America was rapidly deserting the farm for cities. The farm became revered as the symbol of honesty, integrity, diligence and an independent frontier spirit.

Welshmen in their twenties became stooped, shriveled and gray as they hauled coal from the mines of West Virginia and Pennsylvania, just as they'd done in the mines back home. Irish immigrants, fleeing the potato famines, scooped out mud below the East River to lay the pylons of the Brooklyn Bridge for the unheard-of sum of $2.25 a day. But the price was high. Some got their minds gutted by a strange malady called "the bends" when they worked more than five hours at thirty-five feet below sea level; the deeper and longer they dug, the worse the affliction.

In the Gilded Age, though President McKinley was said to keep his ear so close to the ground that it was full of grasshoppers, a pliable, self-delusory government looked the other way. Counseled by captains of industry, the government granted enormous subsidies in the form of restrictive tariffs on foreign goods (which is one way Andrew Carnegie got rich) or land giveaways (which benefited railroad magnates Edward H. Harriman, Leland Stanford, Collis P. Huntington, Charles Crocker and Mark Hopkins).

The manner of smoking a cigar—the elegance of gesture, the ritual of brand selection—marked the polished gentleman from the uncouth. Cigar box labels, exquisitely colored and designed, stretched across tobacconists' display cases to capture the male fancy; they conveyed, in a glance, historical events and the fantasies of the Victorian era, brilliantly portraying its heroes, heroines, sportsmen, journalists, poets, natural wonders, engineering feats.

The spell is broke, the charm
  is flown,
Thus is it with life's fitful fever.
We madly smile when we
  should groan,
Delirium is our best deceiver.

Each lucid interval and
  thought
Recalls the woes of nature's
  charter,
And he that acts as wise men
  ought,
But lives as saints, has died a
  martyr.

  —By J. Mosier for Byron Cigars,
  1902

Questionable labor practices were not discussed at proper dinner parties, and a wife, though she was the moral guardian of the family, learned not to probe too deeply. Newspapers and magazines rarely alluded to industrial or business improprieties, since their owners could be counted among the perpetrators.

By no means was the Victorian businessman left alone to grapple with such affairs of conscience. The Word of God and Word of Man were ever ready at his elbow. Henry Ward Beecher had thundered on the Fourth of July in 1876: "The laborer ought to be ashamed of himself who in twenty years does not own the ground on which his house stands . . . who has not in that house provided carpets for the rooms, who has not his China plates, who has not his chromos, who has not some books nestling on the shelf." Carroll D. Wright of the Massachusetts Bureau of Labor Statistics, in a speech to factory owners, declared that rich and powerful manufacturers were "instruments of God for the upbuilding of the human race."

Even with these support systems, making money was a risky, alienating business. The cyclical nature of financial panics, which seemed to occur every decade, was little understood and far different from the

In the 1870s, one journalistic wag counted the millionaires on a Saratoga Springs veranda and calculated that their combined worth would settle half the national debt. Below (left to right), Pullman, Leiter, Gage, Armour, Rockefeller and Carnegie are grouped at table on a cigar box label.

farm. There a man had only the vicissitudes of nature to grapple with, and could share his anguish with fellow farmers gathered round the cracker barrel. In the new industrial world, there was no such collegiality. The need for personal reassurance and stability in the fast-changing world was great.

So, by the mid-1800s, gentlemen of all social stripes were organizing into clubs. They formed civic, charitable, college and professional associations. The YMCA was founded in 1851, the Grange in 1867, the Elks in 1868. When the Rotary Club was organized in 1902, members called each other by

LITTLE SCOUT

LITTLE SCOUT

CENTRE RUS.

COLLEGE DAYS   COLLEGE DAY

COLLEGE DAYS   COLLEGE DAY

"*There is a magic in the memory of schoolboy friendship: it softens the heart and even affects the nervous system of those who have no heart.*"
—Benjamin Disraeli, novelist and Prime Minister to Queen Victoria

DETROIT FREE PRESS

NEWSBOY CIGARS.

MANUFACTURED BY
BROWN BROTHERS CO.
DETROIT.

Sir Thomas Lipton, the quintessential Victorian rags-to-riches British millionaire, began with one grocery store and ended up heading a provisions empire that included meat-packing houses in Chicago, fruit farms, jam factories and bakeries in England, and tea, coffee and cacao plantations in Ceylon. Like many of his peers, Lipton embraced the costly sport of yachting, entering the prestigious America's Cup Races five times between 1899 and 1930.

In 1901, three years after having been knighted, Lipton stated: "There is nothing in the world I want more than that cup." But the cup eluded him. In his last entry, in 1930, he lost in four straight races to Harold "Mike" Vanderbilt. He died in 1931, best known for the tea that bears his name. To yachtsmen, however, he will always be remembered as a dedicated racing sailor and gentleman.

their first names, a custom that survives today. Small towns formed volunteer fire departments; to be one of "our fire laddies" was prestigious then, as it is now. By 1910 there were 400 fraternal organizations in America, with a collective membership of nine million.

At their exclusive social clubs, the Old Guard drank, smoked, talked and dined without the company of women. The Union Club of New York, the oldest social club in America, was organized in 1836; Boston's Somerset Club followed in 1851, the Newport (Rhode Island) Reading Room in 1853, the Cosmos Club in Washington in 1878, San Francisco's Bohemian Club in 1882. All are currently listed in the Social Register.

Gentlemen of means also gave black-tie at-home bachelor dinners for each other. At Edward Linley Sambourne's men-only dinner for twelve guests on July 11, 1893, two chefs and two menservants prepared and served the following: caviar, clear soup, cold salmon, chaud-froid pigeons, tomato salad, roast lamb, peas, haricots verts, anchovy savory cream cheese, ices, pineapple cream, roast chicken, Russian salad, jellied macedoine of fruit; and grapes, cherries and Green Gage plums. The gentlemen, Mrs. Sambourne reported in her diary, carried on till two in the morning, consuming twenty-two bottles of wine and twelve bottles of champagne. The menu, staggering by most standards, was usual party fare among the socially élite. Most Victorian men overate, overdrank,

"The anxiety attending this race is deep and earnest," wrote the London Times Special Correspondent as the yacht America prepared to challenge England's Royal Yacht Squadron in 1844. Two days later, the British yachting establishment at Cowes was forced to acknowledge America's staggering victory. Her owner, Commodore Stevens, took possession of the ornate silver urn that would thereafter be known as the America's Cup, and Queen Victoria boarded the yacht with Prince Albert for an official visit. The New York Yacht Club became the cup's new home, thus establishing the fiercely competitive America's Cup Races.

CUP DEFENDER

and were dead by sixty-five. (Grover Cleveland, president in the 1880s, was nicknamed Uncle Jumbo. He weighed 260 pounds when he died at the age of sixty-six.)

Although Victorians were hard gamblers and drinkers, gentlemen were expected to hold their liquor in mixed company, to be gallant with proper ladies and circumspect with those who were not. On the town by themselves, gentlemen were drawn by tinny music emanating from dance halls, the flick of diamond earbobs under a street lamp, the flash of black lace stockings nested in layers of petticoats. They savored fleeting flirtations with chanteuses and music hall dancers; the more daring and desperate formed semipermanent liaisons. In proper families, there was always the fear that a son would stray too far into the shadowy maw of the theater.

In all social classes men were expected to be avid sportsmen. If one were rich, sailing, polo, horse racing, and riding to the hounds—all sports requiring substantial skill and money— were *de rigueur*. Golf and tennis, both nineteenth-century inventions imported from England, were first embraced by the upper class. And though building a grass court had never been cheap, by the 1880s tennis had seeped down to the middle class. (In the 1970s, when the head groundskeeper at Wimbledon was asked what it took to keep the grass courts

ONE OF A KIND

After inheriting the New York *Herald* from his father at age twenty-five, the flamboyant James Gordon Bennett went on to sponsor Stanley's expedition to find Livingstone (successful) and the *Jeannette*'s voyage to the Arctic in 1879 (unsuccessful). But his real love was sports, on which he spent an estimated $30 million. An eminent polo player and yachtsman, he also provided backing for balloon, airplane and auto races on both sides of the Atlantic.

Still a bachelor at the age of thirty-eight, Bennett scotched his impending nuptials by relieving himself in the fireplace at his fiancée's New Year's Day party. New York's Four Hundred closed ranks against him, and he lived out most of his final years in France.

in prime condition, he replied: one hundred years of manure and one hundred years of rolling.)

Running down the social scale were: rowing, basketball, baseball (the National Game by the 1880s), bowling, boxing and wrestling. Everybody, even women, played billiards and rode bicycles.

All men hunted and fished, the social distinction being where one engaged in the sport. The poor fished and hunted where they always have: along creeks and rivers and in their neighbor's back forty. The very rich had their "camps" in the Adirondacks and Lake George in upstate New York. After Buffalo Bill romanticized the American cowboy, the wealthy journeyed west to dude ranches in Wyoming and the Rockies. In wintertime, they headed for grouse country in the mountains of North Carolina, where George Vanderbilt had constructed his mighty social fortress, the Biltmore.

With steadily mounting wealth and seduced by the heady tenor of the times, Victorians flocked to gambling. Fortunes were won and lost overnight in high-stakes games of faro, poker, roulette, and all manner of sports events—boxing, horse racing, wrestling, sailing.

First "opening its doors to Satan" in 1819, when city fathers winked at billards, unchaperoned dancing and private gambling, Saratoga Springs had no peer when it

"Of course, a man who is much talked about is always very attractive. One feels there must be something in him, after all."

—*Cecily, speaking to Algernon in* The Importance of Being Earnest *by Oscar Wilde*

came to the social station and inventiveness of its gamblers. Millionaires at the Springs dreamed up a new gambling game called Fly-lo, in which each player would set a cube of sugar saturated with honey in front of him at the dining table, place his bet, and then wait to see which cube would first attract a fly. With the arrival in 1861 of John Morrissey, a huge, brawling, handsome Irish immigrant boxer, gambling was seriously—and openly—launched. At his Matilda Street club, Morrissey took cash only and barred women and local citizens from gaming. He was enormously successful, he gave large sums to charity and closed his doors on Sunday, but no blueblood dowagers ever welcomed him and his dazzling, dark-eyed bride across the thresholds of their Broadway mansions.

Morrissey, cut to the quick, simply poured more energy into his trade. By the 1870s, rich carpetbaggers from the South, Nevada silver lode mining kings and the Eastern establishment industrial aristocracy all jostled for preferred places at his gam-

While the men took their chances with Lady Luck, Victorian women at Saratoga followed the schedule spelled out in an 1868 visitors' guide: "For a lady: rise and dress; go down to the spring; drink to the music of the band; walk round the park; bow to gentlemen and chat a little . . . see who comes in on the train; take a siesta; walk in the parlors . . . have some gossip with ladies; dress for dinner . . ."

bling events. Capitalizing on the Victorian appetite for sports, he built the Springs' first racetrack and sponsored boat racing on Lake Saratoga. Despite his efforts, Morrissey died at age forty-seven, porcine and worn out from overeating and other excesses, without ever having gained the social acceptance he so coveted.

His replacement was the dapper, elegant Richard Canfield, who came to be called the Prince of Gambling. Canfield bought Morrissey's club and redecorated it, much as it can be seen today, with red-flocked wallpaper, moon-globe chandeliers, green satin draperies and cabbage-rose carpets. Importing the best chefs from France, he charged higher prices than New York's Delmonico's and Sherry's, and called his new place the Casino. Soon, ten gambling houses were imitating his success. The roulette wheels and dice clattered round the clock.

Prodded by local citizens and sensing the circulation bonanza to be

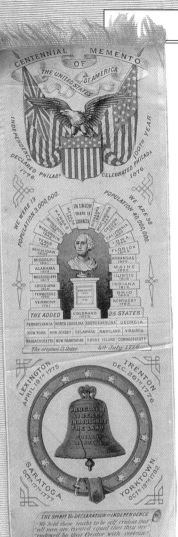

found in the high-life scandal of bluebloods, veteran news-paperman Joseph Pulitzer sent his star reporter, Nellie Bly, to expose the debaucheries of Saratoga. In August of 1894, the headlines of her story blazed across the pages of the New York *World*: "Money mad by night and day/Little children who play horses." The subhead was no less irate: "Reputable and disreputable women, solid merchants, bankers, touts, criminals and race track riff-raff crazed by the mania for gold."

The heyday would soon be over.

By the late 1890s, jingoism and a policy of expansion led the new nation to rattle its sabers on behalf of Cuba and her fight for independence from Spain. When the *Maine* was blown up in Havana harbor in April 1898, the American government demanded that Spain withdraw from Cuba; Spain refused, of course, and declared war. At the Treaty of Paris nine months later, the United States acquired Puerto Rico, Guam and the Philippines, earning a select place at the table of imperialistic world powers.

The Spanish-American War also catapulted the dashing Teddy Roosevelt to national prominence, remembered for his rallying cry "Remember the *Maine*!" as the Rough Riders charged up San Juan Hill. It would take Roosevelt to steer antitrust laws through Congress and thus change forever the unfettered manly pursuit of making money. But the real death knell was the Sixteenth Amendment, which introduced the personal income tax in 1913. Never again would the art of making money freewheel so wildly across the imaginations of men.

ROMANTIC NOTIONS

HEARTS AND FLOWERS
THE SOCIAL GRACES
THE TIE THAT BINDS

Forget me not!
'Tis all I ask of thee,
Preserve one spot
In your heart for me.

"We both felt, while bought bobbles are more immediately attractive, our hearts warm more to the home-made offering . . . lace bags in a rainbow of colors, filled with lavendar from the garden and tied with a ribbon . . .

—Maud Humphrey, in The Illustrated Diary of a Victorian Woman, 1890

"Love should run out to meet love with open arms. Indeed, the ideal story is that of two people who go into love step for step, with a fluttered consciousness, like a pair of children venturing together into a dark room."
—From Virginibus Puerisque by Robert Louis Stevenson

In an era of wild expansion, immense opportunities stretched across the land. Change was everywhere. And if change occasioned uncertainties, romantic notions helped to cloak them. Romantic notions floated on dreams, buoyed by the prosperity of the times.

So Victorians sang songs that romanticized the life and youth they'd left behind. *She's Only a Bird in a Gilded Cage, I Dream of Jeannie with the Light Brown Hair* and *When the Corn Is Waving, Annie* were three favorites. They wrote honey-dipped poetry to each other, sent greeting cards and nosegays of garden flowers. On holidays and birthdays they delivered Aunt Sarah's never-fail chocolate cake, penned commemorative poems and essays. Under the lamplight of a winter's night, children pasted mementoes into scrapbooks. Mothers displayed keepsakes on whatnot shelves and wrote letters to far-flung sons. In the pain of separation, remembering was important.

For Victorians, flowers and nature symbolized the spiritual, the ideal, all that was sunny and beautiful and eternally young. Representing this bucolic fancy, the London School of Faerie Painting portrayed winsome children in flowered costumes as ethereal messengers from a world of myth and romance—a fantasy world untouched by science and fact.

But the world of myth and romance swirled most intensely about Victorian women. Stuck on pedestals, the ladies were flattered by the poetry of Yeats, Wordsworth, the Rossettis, the Brownings; elevated as tragic heroines in the novels of George Sand, Flaubert, the Brontës; sentimentalized in Puccini operas. Women were portrayed as Pre-Raphaelite madonnas with flowers in their hair and as Columbia, the patriotic, pure protectress of the Union, surrounded by sheaves of wheat. Maxfield Parrish painted them as goddesses in diaphanous gowns, reclining on ancient verandas; Mary Cassatt, as symbols of nurturing Motherhood. Sculptor Daniel Chester

As gifts of friendship, love tokens were frequently exchanged among men and women: small baubles—a hair comb, a ring, a bracelet or a locket with an appropriate motto inside. A gold hand-cuff locked on the wrist "of the fair recipient by a gentleman," wrote Godey's in 1833, was "a curious but not uncommon conceit."

A perfect Woman, nobly
  plann'd
To warn, to comfort and
  command;
And yet a Spirit still, and
  bright
With something of angelic
  light.
  —From William Wordsworth's
  "A Perfect Woman"

Unable to obtain high-quality paper in America, Esther Howland imported linen papers from England to make the lace for her valentines. Her chef d'oeuvres, with as many as seven layers of paper lace attached by a painted satin heart, cost $50 apiece.

By and large, valentine-making was a cottage industry. Women pasted scraps, artificial flowers, lace papers, ribbons and feathers, and attached bits of mirror or tassels following a prescribed pattern. Assemblers who demonstrated talent were free to construct cards according to their own design. Wages were low. A girl might work for six months for the price of one of her creations.

Flowers, whether picked by a child
from the garden or delivered in an elegant silver cornucopia, were perennial
gifts of affection in Victorian America
—mixing honied scents with sentiments of the heart.

Love's Captive

French chiseled them into marble monuments of justice. In park fountains, on state seals and on the façades of Beaux-Arts buildings, the female figure represented knowledge, sovereignty, peace and order.

For Victorian ladies and their lovers, no day was more sentimental than Valentine's Day. The ladies sent forth billets-doux in scented envelopes, painted with scenes of lovebirds and garlands, while gentlemen entwined their poetic sentiments with ribbons, paper lace and lacquered roses trimmed with gold tassels. In the golden era of valentines, the 1840s, a heartsick swain could send a penny valentine or one for thirty dollars, a handmade, seven-page lace masterpiece studded with seed pearls and velvet pansies. A bashful, inarticulate lover could buy a "valentine writer," a collection of popular love poems, choosing the appropriate message to send to the object of his or her affections. Valentines also marked other circumstances, happy and unhappy: arrivals, departures, unrequited love. Comic, rude and pornographic valentines were sent to town cranks and philanderers.

The high priestess of American valentines was a most unlikely candidate. Esther Howland, a graduate of Mount Holyoke Seminary, had received her first English-made valentine when she was nineteen years old. Enthralled, she began to make her own paper-and-lace confections,

Cupid's roving, plucking roses,
Lo! in one a bee reposes.
Bending o'er to nearer view it,
He was stung before he knew it.
What a cute idea cried Cupid,
Hitherto I've been stupid;
In a rose, I, too, will tarry,
Till rose and me a maid shall carry.
When we rest above her heart
I may ply my poison dart!
—George Birdseye, in *Godey's Lady's Book*

displaying them in her father's bookstore in Worcester, Massachusetts. Within weeks orders amounting to five thousand dollars were rolling in. A stunned Esther was in business.

On the airy third floor of the family's spacious home, Esther organized an assembly line of girls—mostly friends and relatives—who attached the valentine components of small colored images and paper lace. Each year Esther added fancier and more expensive novelties, such as hand-painted satin hearts, silk flowers, glazed paper wafers. As the valentines moved off the assembly line, none could be boxed without Esther's inspection. By the 1870s, annual sales of the Howland enterprise, which now included greeting cards of all kinds, had reached $100,000. Esther was the rarest of Victorian creatures, a rich, respected business woman.

Love tokens—trinkets, fans, gloves, jeweled clasps and combs, silver Bible cases—were sent on all occasions. Often, feelings were expressed in the form of flowers. According to the 1870 edition of *Flowers: Their Language and Poetry*, each flower and its position in a bouquet represented a particular sentiment. Presented upside down, a flower carried a negative message. A rosebud with leaves and thorns intact could engender both hope and fear in the bosom of the loved one. Stripped of thorns, it offered the most sanguine of messages; deprived of its blossom and with thorns remaining, the flower's message was unmistakably clear—the loved one was no longer loved.

Friendships were prized in a new light, since so many were newly formed in this land of mobility. The clasped hand, the icon of friendship, was exchanged as a token of esteem, printed on notepapers and fashioned into wedding rings.

"There is no happiness comparable to that of the first handclasp, when one asks 'Do you love me?' and the other replies 'Yes.'"
—From Bel Ami, by Guy de Maupassant

By the 1870s greeting cards had become increasingly elaborate, with pullout tabs, popups and movable parts. To enhance the mystery of a card, the name of its sender could be concealed under decorated flaps with hinges. Candies, sachets and even musical box movements were buried under lace ribbon and feathers. In one card, the vest of a gentleman whose love is unrequited opens to reveal a great wounded, dripping heart.

The camaraderie among women was touching and strong. Left alone with large families for long days, wives nourished one another with advice and gossip, confided their innermost secrets and exchanged passionate letters. No longer isolated on farms, they swapped recipes and herbal remedies over the backyard fence, shared the joys and anguish of child-rearing. At potluck suppers and church socials, they began to band together to correct the evils afflicting their communities: drunkenness in their menfolk, exploitation of women in sweatshops and factories, child labor in mines and textile mills. In July of 1848, when they convened at Seneca Falls, New York, their Declaration of Sentiments (how delicately Victorian the title) was essentially a call for women's rights. Elizabeth Cady Stanton, Lucretia Mott and Susan B. Anthony became household words.

Most women continued to place the highest value on their roles as wives and mothers. Women were the chief arrangers of their family's social affairs, a critical component in "getting ahead," and to them fell the lot of sustaining that most vital of Victorian traditions: social climbing. The rules were elaborate and complex. One moved gingerly through a web of subtleties. There were people one associated with, and people one did not associate with. Once, calling on friends had meant a joyous exchange of gossip, recipes, and the fashion news in hats and fans. But as the century moved from simple to complex, from rural to urban, and strangers assaulted the "old, understood decencies," a rigid formality evolved around the social call. It was a duty and a way of getting ahead—an "old girl" network of sorts.

Today the postal service estimates that greeting cards constitute half the first-class mail sent in the United States—a trend that began with the long distances and depersonalization that characterized the new industrialized society.

For upper-class matrons, making two or three visits in an afternoon was usual, each lasting twenty or thirty minutes. It was gauche to call upon a person outside one's own social class, or outside the customary calling hours of the "at home" day of the recipient. Failing to return a visit, no matter how distasteful, was a social gaffe of the highest order. Cakes and tea could be served, but one must take care not to put on airs by serving fare elegant beyond one's means. A male presence, while generally raising the tone of conversation, inhibited meaningful gossip—which, after all, was what the social call was all about.

A calling card, smelling faintly of violets and left on a silver tray, spelled excitement and promise. It was also studded with pitfalls. To the *cognoscenti*, a card could be a fatal indicator of one's breeding. "Its texture should be fine; its engraving, a plain script; its size not too large or small to attract attention in either way," advised *Godey's* in the late 1870s.

Equally elaborate were the rules regarding introductions, which could properly be made only by an accepted member of the same social class. But who was an acceptable member? One's ten-year-old sister was not; a maiden auntie was. The lines were blurred. One trod carefully. By the 1880s, the handshake had fallen from general use. Thus a lady on the street would accord a gentleman a faint smile or formal bow; under no condition would she address him without an intro-

To fashionable Victorians, one's visiting card was a subtle indication of breeding. A card should be neither too large or garish nor too small to call attention to itself. Despite the popularity of illustrated cards portraying flowers, pets and current events, such as the Philadelphia Centennial or the Chicago World's Fair, in better circles only a plain script on the best-quality, cream-white paper was used.

duction. Upon her invitation, the gentleman might join her, but they must walk sufficiently far apart so that "a dog might pass between them." A gentleman would assist a lady over rough spots by placing his hand under her elbow. After dark, or if she was ill or feeble, she might ask for the assistance of his full arm and remain within the bounds of propriety.

To lend stability to wobbly social positions, another Victorian romantic notion was born: instant heraldic crests. Overnight, symbols and Latin phrases were chosen and affixed to family china, silver and carriage doors. Crests were embroidered onto family linens by nuns, handsomely paid for creating such instant heirlooms. Manufacturing one's history would have been unthinkable in England, but no one in America really minded. It was all a splendid game, and the most important thing was knowing the rules.

In courtship, on both sides of the Atlantic, love matches were encouraged only within one's class. When love and marriage were incompatible, rectifying the two could pose a terrible dilemma. The worst possibility was

Fans, subtle instruments of flirtation, were also used to instruct and advertise.

that a daughter might "throw herself at a nobody," thus ruining years of painstaking preparation. It was a mother's nightmare.

One nineteenth-century female novelist compared the London season to a slave market. But to the pretty young women who were "coming out," being presented to society meant freedom to travel alone, a new wardrobe, autonomy, excitement. At the beginning of the 1894 London season, one daughter confided to her mother in a letter written on the eve of a country weekend: "I have just come from the garden where I have gathered such

> You never saw anything so fine
> As Princess Clementine's valentine!
> It glittered with gold; it shimmered with lace;
> Pink Cupids poised with dainty grace,
> Plump of limb and sly of face;
> Poems and posies, garlands gay,
> Were mixed in a decorative way.
> Attached to the rose with this billet-doux:
> "No knife can cut our love in two."
>
> —Tudor Jenks, in *St. Nicholas Magazine*

a bunch of lovely roses to wear tonight. . . . I mean to enjoy it like anything, not knowing what will happen amongst all those millionaires. Hardly any of them have less than seven thousand a year. So darling, your little own may have a chance of fishing out one of them. . . . What a grab there will be when dinner-time comes."

Like most of life's ceremonies in the Victorian world, customs of courtship and marriage were carefully hedged in with propriety. The higher the social class, the higher the hedges. Among the upper class courtship was meticulously monitored, with engagements usually lasting from six months to two years. During this period each family passed the prospective bride or groom through such finely screened considerations as

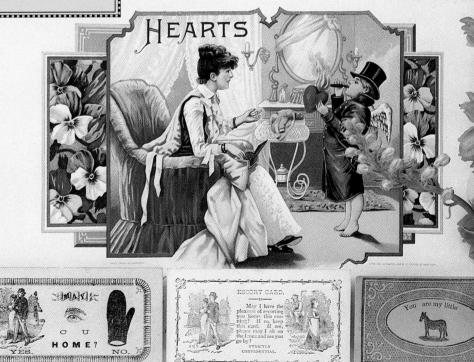

lineage, social and political connections, and wealth. Real wealth was best, but even a penniless young man could be considered a suitable suitor if he were sufficiently intelligent and had a promising future.

For a woman, plain or beautiful, a substantial dowry or "settlement" always enhanced her marital desirability. One could be "settled upon" with a sum of money or a handsome gift, such as a well-appointed house in the "right" neighborhood. Such a gift would simultaneously demonstrate to the world the level of social aspirations of the young couple, and the satisfaction of the bride's family with the impending nuptials. Sometimes being "settled upon" was a verbal agreement, an affair of honor; sometimes it required a legal document, as in the case of royalty or where great sums of money were involved.

In the earlier part of the century, one's church affiliation—which was also linked to social status—mattered greatly. But as Victorian society became increasingly secular, the importance of religion lessened.

Once betrothed, the bridal pair was welcomed to the inner

The almanac of flowers, above, came from London's distinguished House of Rimmel, perfumer par excellence. At 96 Strand Street, Eugene Rimmel produced a dazzling selection of soaps, perfumes and love tokens. Tucked away in two fashionable seventeenth-century row houses, ladies assembled packets of perfume, soaps, sachets; pearl-handled lace fans, golden charms, satin neckties, headdresses of feathers and ribbons, Japanese ornamental hairpins; filigree crosses set with Bohemian garnets, pearls, topazes; velvet-covered musical glove boxes (since the seventeenth century, gloves were considered an appropriate St. Valentine's Day gift); and, of course, valentines. No wonder fancy boxes from the House of Rimmel, delivered to maidens from St. Petersburg to Calcutta, could cause hearts to skip a beat!

sanctum of each family. With a united front to the world, all disagreements were shelved; the couple was fêted publicly, nourished privately, and their mutual fortunes advanced in every possible way. To their delight, the lovers could now stroll alone, hold hands, even go off during the day for a carriage ride unchaperoned. At nightfall or on overnight country weekends, however, the pair dutifully separated.

For her April wedding in London in 1898, Maud Sambourne chose white muslin dresses with sky-blue sashes for her bridesmaids, and white hats trimmed with ostrich plumes. Her trousseau, lavish for the upper middle class, included eight night dresses of lawn hand-embroidered by nuns, dozens of day dresses, blouses, undergarments, and the all-important traveling dress of shot heliotrope voile, a matching sleeveless coat lined with heliotrope silk, and the *pièce de résistance*—a rustic straw hat trimmed with mauve lilac branches and draperies of heliotrope chiffon. But then, how could she even consider packing a smaller wardrobe when her honeymoon abroad was to last six weeks and would include bookings at Europe's most fashionable hotels in Monte Carlo, Paris, Florence and Venice?

Even though she was marrying a rich, handsome merchant prince, on the eve of her engagement Maud expressed misgivings. Not so much about the impending marriage, but about her loss of freedom. Since "coming out," she had had many beaux; traveled

ALL LOVE IS SWEET, GIVEN OR RETURNED.

unchareroned to the fanciest of country houses; received a commodious allowance for clothing and entertainment; and was free for the first time in her life to pursue her own interests without parental direction. Once she was married, her precious freedom would again be subject to the approval of another—this time her husband.

But Maud, age twenty-three, was nearing the marriageable danger point. She had been eighteen when she was presented to society. To marry *too* quickly would have raised questions: Why so eager, so hasty to take the first offer that came along? To wait beyond the age of twenty-five raised a new set of questions: Was she being too particular to consider someone seriously? Or—and this was the worst—was there no one to consider?

In America, at least for the middle class, marital requirements were more flexible. While families sought compatible matches for their children, options were broader. Affairs of the heart were given greater credence. While social class was important, it was as much a matter of shared values as it was genealogy. A couple could marry early or late, but were expected to weigh the advantages of each.

In her "Home Interest" column in *The Brooklyn Magazine*, Mrs. Henry Ward Beecher advocated early marriages to prevent young lovers from yielding to temptation, and from becoming so fixed in their ways that they could not "yield kindly to one another's wishes or peculiarities."

She also advocated late marriages to permit a young woman to complete her education, and to make certain that a young

> *"I think you good, gifted, lovely; a fervent, a solemn passion is conceived in my heart; it leans to you; draws you to my center and spring of life, wraps my existence about you—kindling in pure powerful flame, fuses you and me in one."*
> —From Jane Eyre, by Charlotte Brontë

man's business prospects were secure. When she wrote her column, in 1889, the median age for marriage in the United States was thirty years for men, and twenty for women, although marriage in rural communities tended to occur earlier, last longer and produce more children. The young couples took their marriage vows quite seriously. In 1890, only 33,416 in 542,537 marriages ended in divorce.

Finding a suitable mate in the cities was an acute problem for young men and women. Proper meeting places were few: churches and intellectual events, such as lectures, Bible study and debating societies, were considered safe; social clubs, whose doings were covered in minute detail in local society columns, were open to greater question. But for all newly arrived greenhorns, particularly women, the freedom of city life was fraught with danger. Involvement with a married

"Be shy of loving frankly; never tell all you feel or (a better way still) feel very little. . . . Get yourselves married as they do in France, where the lawyers are the bridesmaids and confidants. Never . . . make any promises which you cannot at any required moment command and withdraw. That is the way to get on and be respected, and have a virtuous character."
—William Makepeace Thackeray in Vanity Fair

Bid happiness
return to me
By telling me that not in vain
Is all the love I feel for thee,
Say this, and I can smile again.

Down the waters of life we'll float,
Hand in hand in our little boat,
Till all the billows of life are passed
And we rest for ever, our anchor cast.

Your wedding day is bright and gay.
You're happy, I believe you,
My wish is this: May all this bliss
Ne'er for a moment leave you.

a Fellow for every day in the week.

Nobody cares for the man in the moon,
He may see what he likes all night.
How can he remain so placid and calm
In the midst of such scenes of delight!

I've come to bring this little ring,
I'll put it, sweetheart, on your hand,
The days will pass, and soon my lass,
Before the altar we will stand.

Queen of my heart, as I gaze in your eyes,
Those eyes of the deepest of blue,
This garden appears like a sweet Paradise,
A Garden of Eden with you.

man was cause for scandal; being pregnant out of wedlock, cause for banishment.

Weddings were usually held in churches, followed by receptions in the bride's home or garden. Claret punch, champagne, platters of tea cakes, sweetmeats and pastries were served. Depending on the finances of the bride's family, an elaborate, seated dinner with ten to twelve courses and appropriate wines for each would be served.

After the 1870s, when railroads and transatlantic steamships linked cities to romantic spas and grand hotels, newlywed couples traveled far on their honeymoons, luxuriating in bridal suites on Mississippi riverboats, at Saratoga Springs, White Sulphur Springs, at Chicago's Palmer House, the Palace in San Francisco, New York's Plaza Hotel and Niagara Falls, which of course became the honeymoon capital.

The young couple embarked grandly upon their life together in this most heady of times.

DIVERSIONS

PARLOR ENTERTAINMENTS
MUSICAL PASTIMES
FÊTES AND FESTIVITIES

Entertainment for the Victorian family was, by and large, homemade and homespun. Pastimes could be as simple as small talk on the porch of a summer evening, or parlor games of tiddly-winks, old maid and jack straws, a forerunner of pick-up sticks. There was hopscotch and jumping double-dutch in the schoolyard, or rolling jacks and shooting marbles in a dusty ring under an elm tree. Nature fringed the edges of every small town, so there were picnics along the river, fishing in the creek, swimming in water holes, butterflies to be caught, spring violets to be gathered, cidering and nutting parties in the fall. Winter brought sledding, and ice skating on reed-rimmed ponds.

For boys there were lead soldiers and celluloid cutout villages with farmhouse, gardens and general store to be constructed. For girls there were doll houses, ranging from elaborate store-bought wonders that sold for $100 unfurnished to grocery boxes glued together and equipped with homemade furniture, curtains and wallpapers. After 1845, German printers began to produce *bilderbogen*, paper dolls in printed sheets. By the 1860s, celebrity paper dolls such as Topsy and Little Eva from *Uncle Tom's Cabin* had become the rage.

Many were the evenings that mother and child spent meticulously arranging "scrap"—glossy, colorful cutouts of animals, flowers, mythical creatures and fairy-tale characters—and pasting it into keepsake albums that would become family heirlooms. Sometimes the albums were used as learning tools, teaching the alphabet, or spelling, or the classification of animals or plants. Ladies applied scrap to needle cases, fire screens, glass jars, chairs and clocks. They even decorated the insides of cupboards and "glory," or gift boxes of wood and papier-mâché, layering scrap, foil, fabric and milliners' labels in pleasing combinations.

As a hearthtime activity for mothers and children, pasting scrap into albums could be compared with putting together a family photo album today. Scissors, paste, imagination, a sense of order, an aesthetic eye and occasional wit combined to make delightful commentary on Victorian life. Such albums are highly prized by today's collectors of ephemera.

While Edison's phonograph, Kinetoscope and Vitagraph changed the cultural life in America, the telephone and telegraph revolutionized business.

H ardly a household was without its concertina, its pump organ or piano in the front parlor, where special occasions were celebrated with duets and rounds of singing. Among upper-class families, evening musicales were elaborate, formal events, with twelve to sixteen guests carefully chosen for their social and professional compatibility. Days of planning went into the musical arrangements, the décor and the dinner menu, which often ran to ten courses with appropriate wines, champagne and claret. After dinner, according to custom, ladies left the gentlemen to their cigars and port. Two rounds were permissible before the gentlemen joined the ladies in the parlor, where hired musicians sang to piano or violin accompaniment. Guests of a musical bent, who had arrived with sheet music modestly concealed under their cloaks, hoped to be asked to play. They usually were.

Concertos by Liszt, the waltzes of Richard Strauss,

Paper dollies came in families, each dressed in the haute couture of the time. Sheets of paper dolls inserted into magazines, a concept introduced by Godey's, were followed by sheets of chromolithographic scrap. Paper soldiers for boys, in the garb of U.S. Rough Riders, British Highlanders or the colorful Zouaves, were made to be cut out, pasted on cardboard stands and moved about in dress parades.

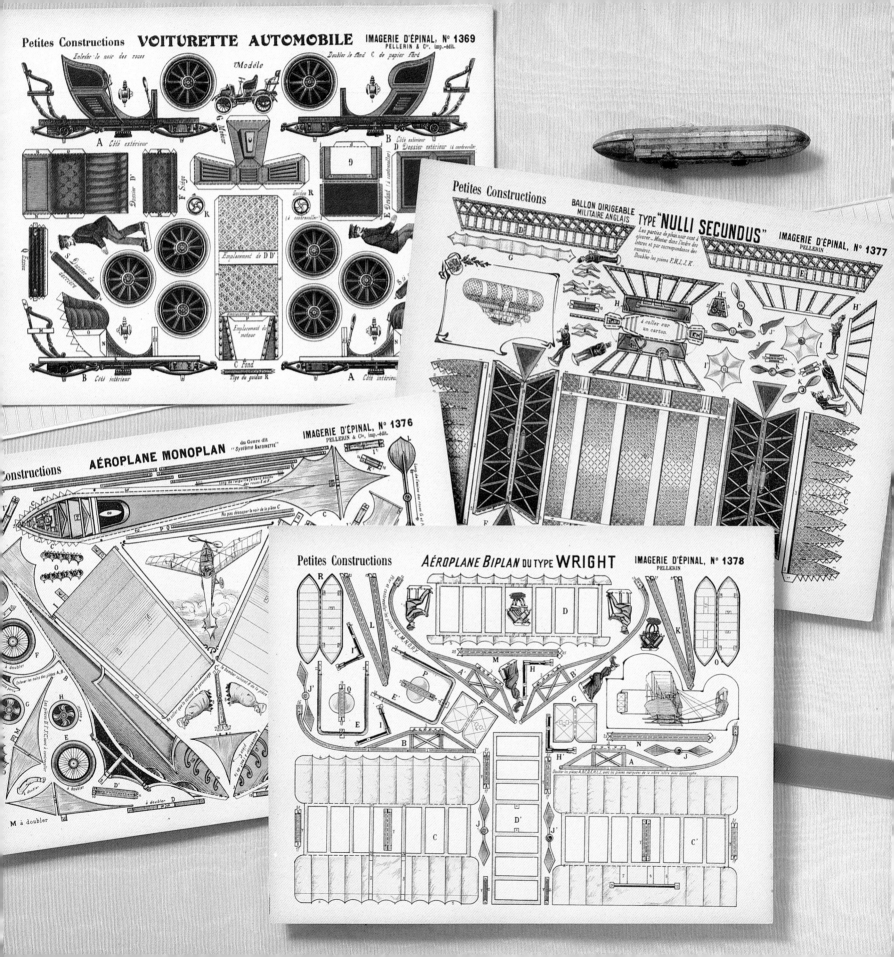

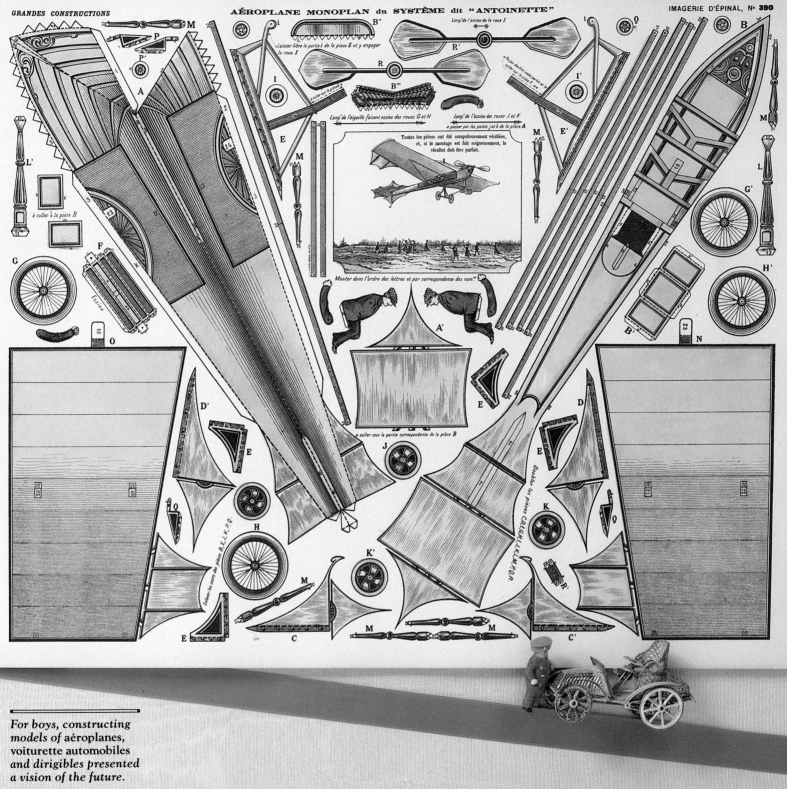

For boys, constructing models of aéroplanes, voiturette automobiles and dirigibles presented a vision of the future.

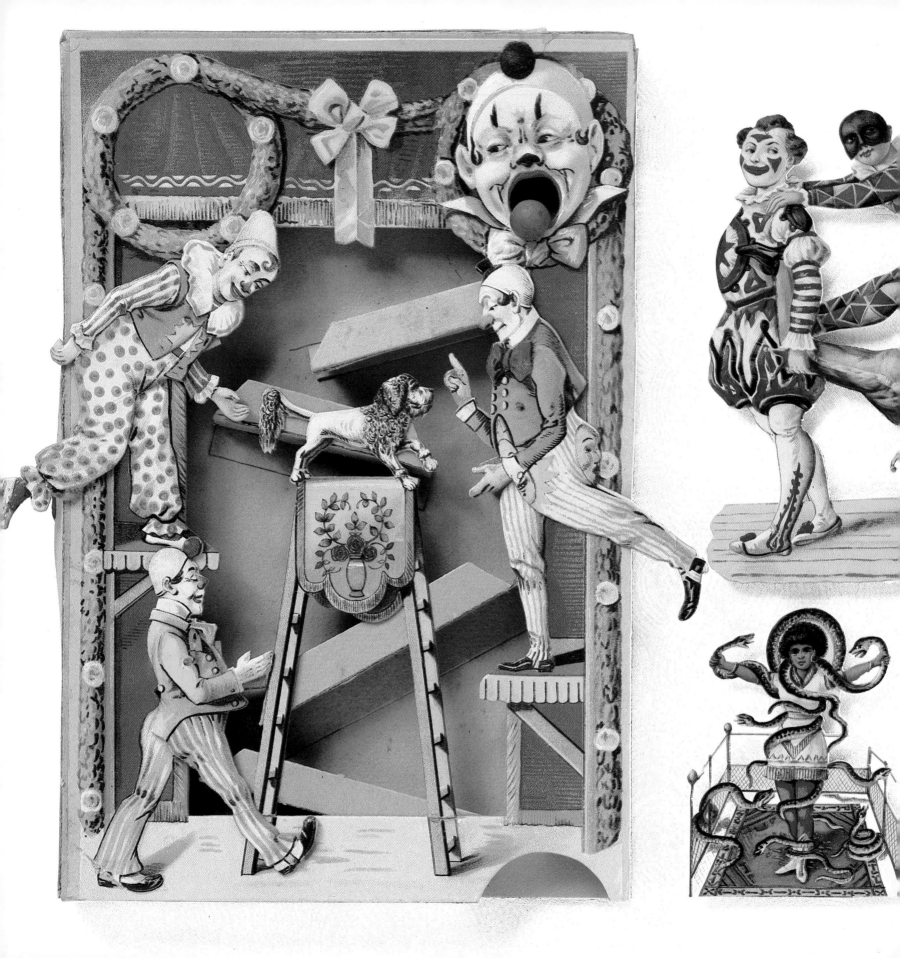

arias from Offenbach and Puccini were highbrow fare. Gilbert and Sullivan quartets were popular, but tricky to sing. *The Mikado*, which opened in New York in 1885, unleashed a mania for all things *japonnaise*—fans and parasols hand-painted with Japanese designs, lampshade embroideries, porcelain and, of course, Nanki-Poo's charming, singable aria, "A Wandering Minstrel, I."

How Victorians adored music! In the larger world, musicians with hurdy-gurdies strolled city streets while their monkeys danced to airs cranked out on small barrel organs. German bands played under grape arbors at outdoor dancing pavilions. Most small towns had a bandshell or tiny opera house for itinerant performers. During winter the town's marching band practiced weekly, bursting forth in spanking new red-and-blue mail-order uniforms for the Fourth of July; then the entire town turned out for the annual march to the cemetery, where they laid wreaths of ivy, daisies, delphinium and sweet william on the graves of the glorious dead. In larger towns, music hall chanteuses belted out nostalgic and racy songs that celebrated sex and unrequited love. *Home Sweet Home* was a perennial favorite; other tunes reflected current events—*The Bloomer Girl Polka* spoofed the social reformer Amelia Bloomer after she had launched her controversial balloon trousers for women.

Music also heralded political rallies and county fairs, each with their regional specialities: clam or corn-shucking contests, log burling, horse and tractor pulls, and hurling "meadow muffins"—dried cow pies that sailed like frisbees. When the circus came to town, puffing, dusty elephants lumbered down Main Street to the stirring strains of Sousa, with clowns cartwheeling alongside. Gypsy fortunetellers,

sweating trapeze artists, patent-medicine hucksters, wild animals in cages, an authentic Wild West Indian or two, all wove the spell of an exotic, faraway world of magic and romance.

Children, much beloved, were the centerpiece of family festivities. Parties for children in a rich household tended to be lavish, with guest lists running as high as fifty. No stops were spared for entertainment. There might be a Punch and Judy show, performing dogs, a talking bird or hurdy-gurdy. At a dining room table covered with white linen, children sipped tea and nibbled sweets. A tea party menu for fifty guests suggests: 1 gallon tea, 1 gallon coffee, 5 quarts sugar, 12 plates thin buttered bread, 3 plum or currant cakes, 2 rice cakes, 4 pounds of biscuits, 18 sponge cakes, 4 dozen small buns. Fruit in season: strawberries, raspberries or gooseberry jam.

Costume parties, like the fancy-dress balls their parents attended, became vogue after Queen Victoria and Albert hosted their first costume ball in 1842. For a children's fancy-dress party, nannies and mamas spent long hours sewing elaborate outfits, historical costumes being most popular. Little cavaliers came in silken breeches and tunics, Lilliputian ladies in satin ball gowns with tiaras made of pasteboard diamonds. Depending on age, dancing might be included, although one nineteenth-century writer advised: "If the majority of the children are boys, they prefer any description of amusement to dancing." *Plus ça change, plus c'est la même-chose.*

Meanwhile, in English great houses and American country seats, upper-class Victorian couples were vying for the liveliest and most important guests to attend their

SARA BERNHARDT.

(Also blank.)
No. 2129.

AT THE CARNIVAL.   Grace and Beauty.

GRAND MASQUERADE
LICK HOUSE
DEC. 28, 1870.

JOHN M. LAWLOR & CO
PROPRIETORS.

AT THE CARNIVAL.   Harlequin and Columbine.

Queen Victoria described music as "a refined accessory to the good life, morally uplifting, softening and purifying the mind."

Young Maennerchor Grand Annual Ball.
Shrove Tuesday, FEB. 26th 1884.
with TABLEAUX.

house parties—analogs of the present-day country house weekends. Gentlemen sported during the day, ladies gossiped, and everybody enjoyed jolly games in the evening, with an occasional midseason fancy-dress ball or garden party.

Toward the turn of the century, home entertainment began to dwindle. Thomas Edison had invented the gramophone and the Vitagraph, a kind of movie projector, and on April 23, 1896, at a theater in Herald Square, the first flickering images of a film were premiered before a spellbound audience. In time a new entertainment industry would produce a star cult, the likes of which such Victorian idols as Jenny Lind and Sarah Bernhardt could never have comprehended.

Every holiday brought its bounty of food, visiting relatives, a sparkling and decorated house, and special "Sunday" dress. While Thanksgiving, Easter and Valentine's Day had their charms, nothing

"THE DIVINE SARAH"

Sarah Bernhardt triumphed as comedienne and tragedienne, but it was her sensational début in *La Dame aux camélias* in 1860 that electrified American theater audiences. Titillated by her love affairs and her seductive, imperious temperament, they followed her every move as she traveled across the country in a private railroad car with fourteen dogs and four cats. When she declared herself "beyond the tyranny of fashion," wearing only dresses that were plain, straight of line, and allowed freedom of body movement, they admired her independence.

Bernhardt managed her own theater in Paris throughout the 1890s. Despite the amputation of her leg following a knee injury, she continued to perform until a year before her death at the age of seventy-nine.

could upstage a Victorian Christmas. When a tinted etching of a decorated Christmas tree at Windsor Castle was published in 1850, the impact was electric. Decorating a *Tannenbaum* became instantly fashionable, spreading from Windsor to London and ultimately to outposts of the British Empire.

Surprisingly, Victorian America was slow to adopt the beloved Christmas customs we relish today. Despite their appreciation of color and love of ceremony, many Victorians considered Santa Claus, decorating a tree, and lighting waxed tapers on Christmas Eve nothing but heathen nonsense. Beneath their flair for theatricality lay a strong and stubborn puritanical streak. The pulpit railed against such hedonistic, irreligious rituals and practices. Singing carols, hanging greens, wassail bowls and Father Christmas, who in England wore pagan-looking Siberian wolfskins, had nothing to do with the Nativity or the spiritual side of the holiday.

These "hedonistic irreligious rituals" first gained a toehold in New York City, where merchants were quick to sense their commercial value. Toy stores, confectioners' shops and German bakeries began

A-CAROLING WE WILL GO…

While candy-filled paper cornucopias, cookies a-glitter with egg white frosting, and other tree decorations were German in origin, adapted from Prince Albert's Windsor *Tannenbaum*, caroling was an English imprint on the American Victorian Christmas. In the cities, carolers usually strolled in groups of three: one caroler to play the fiddle, one to sing, and a third to sell sheet music. Holiday passers-by would pause, purchase, and join the trio, singing a few stanzas before hurrying on their homeward journey.

A Visit to the Snow Queen's Palace.

to stay open late, to festoon their windows with red silk bunting and holly. Holiday shoppers could not resist the cakes, toys and candies displayed under glittering gas-jet lamps, the smells of cinnamon *kuchens* and sweet almond paste. By the 1870s, Macy's department store was putting on a good Christmas show. One window displayed an amphitheater of wax, rag, bisque and hand-painted porcelain dolls imported from Germany, France, Austria, Switzerland and Bohemia. In another window, scenes from *Uncle Tom's Cabin* were composed in a panorama with steam-driven movable parts.

On giving war toys to children, the English Chambers Miscellaney of Useful and Entertaining Tracts advised mid-nineteenth-century parents: "We have remarked that toys of this kind—mimic guns, swords and other military accoutrements of war—are commonly given to children in France, a practice which perhaps tends to nourish a love of war. We hope English parents will avoid this folly, and impart toys only of simply amusing or improving tendency."

Louis Prang, a German printer and émigré, produced the first U.S. Christmas card in his Roxbury, Massachusetts, print shop in 1875. In his national contest for the best Christmas card art in 1880, he offered prizes up to $2,000—an unheard of fortune in Victorian middle-class America.

By the 1880s, the Christmas conquest was complete. Even Boston had capitulated. Victorians now sent one another lavish, chromolithographed Christmas cards or painted their own. They filled silver-paper cornucopias with candies. They decorated Christmas trees with apples, tangerines, walnuts dipped in egg white; strings of popcorn and cranberries; gold-foil "Dresdens" shaped as miniature stars and steamships, elves and fish and birds.

Handmade gifts were conceived months in advance. After whispered conferences behind closed doors and much scurrying about, family members sewed, sawed, knitted, baked, painted and pasted their gifts, which were usually hung on the tree. There might be a pen-wiper in the shape of a waterlily for Aunt Eliza; a knitting bag worked with blue silk floss and matching blue fringe for Emma; a

The mania for that durable stuffed toy, the teddy bear, originated in 1902 when President Teddy Roosevelt—something of a conservationist and ever alert to the publicity value of his actions—refused to shoot a bear cub.

rose potpourri for Cousin Amy, quince jam for Beth; embroidered bed slippers for Papa. And how many book-markers can a mother use? Dozens.

Under the tree were store-bought toys, usually one for each child: a wind-up dancing bear; Logos, an early form of Scrabble, and a precursor of Monopoly called Moneta; penny whistles, pull toys and stuffed animals. But the most wondrous gift of all was Papa's gift to the entire family, a surprise even to Mother: a magic lantern with a four-wick oil lamp and packet of twenty-five hand-tinted slides. The slides told a spooky story, with images of wicked gargoyles and saintly fairies cast upon a nine-foot-square white muslin screen.

Generally, children did not see the tree until Christmas Eve, when the parlor doors were flung open and the tree blazed forth in its full, candle-lit glory. Presents were usually opened then, with Christmas morning reserved for kitchen and church, the latter having been lavishly decorated with evergreens, Easter lilies, roses and, in the 1880s, poinsettia plants.

The traditional Christmas menu depended upon ethnic background and where one lived. Anglophiles favored sirloin of beef or goose. Most American families served an oyster-stuffed turkey, the native bird that had saved the Pilgrims from hunger and in the wild weighed up to thirty pounds. If a family lived on a farm without benefit of an icebox, vegetables that kept well in the root cellar accompanied the turkey—baked squash, mashed turnips and potatoes, sliced cabbage, pickled watermelon rind and, of course, slabs of

Father Christmas, garbed in his long, furred, white, green or black cloak, belonged to England and Germany. America's red-cheeked, white-bearded Santa Claus was born with the illustrations for Clement Moore's "The Night Before Christmas" (1822). Wildly popular, the poem transformed St. Nicholas into the jovial rogue children know and love today.

A MERRY CHRISTMAS

homemade bread and preserves, mince pie or plum pudding.

The pudding was steamed for at least four hours on Christmas morning, its heavenly aroma permeating the house. Plum pudding recipes were legion, and each household had its favorite, but the essential ingredients were bread crumbs, beef suet and raisins, wrapped in muslin and steeped in liqueur for six weeks. And if the heaviness of the plum pudding did not please the diners after a six- or seven-course feast, its presentation did. Doused with brandy, the pudding was lit and carried aloft to the head of the table. With blue flames dancing on the silver tray, it was toasted with oohs and ahhs and blessings.

After naps and a massive kitchen cleanup, by midafternoon the long-rehearsed Christmas program began. Youngsters whispered painfully memorized recitations, twisting in high-button shoes and velvet breeches. Family members played solos on the violin or piano, or composed tableaux, depicting scenes from the Bible or events in history. To close this glorious day, the family gathered around the piano to sing *Silent Night*.

New Year's Day was usually celebrated quietly with small "at home" suppers. At midnight, guests joined hands and circled the dining table singing *Auld Lang Syne*. Even during such a momentous occasion as the launching of a new century, the custom of unmarried ladies tossing the traditional hazelnut in the fire to determine their matrimonial possibilities, encanting "burn or die; crack and fly" took priority.

The lesson of the priority is clear. In the long run, family, friends, the richness of human relations are what really matter.

"Good appetite to all who eat Thanksgiving turkeys, and may our friends assemble before well-filled tables, with families unbroken and grateful, happy hearts."
—*A holiday greeting from Godey's Lady's Book, 1889*

A NEW YEAR'S MEETING

•

Do you know how to get to
   Grandpa's?
I went on New Year's Day.
You climb the hill where the
   pine trees grow,
And Grandpa comes half-way.

He threatens me with his cane
   and says,
"A kiss, or your life, my dear!"
And then with a regular bear
   hug,
I wish him a Happy New Year.

—Tudor Jenks, in *St. Nicholas Magazine*, January 1896

HALLOWE'EN PUMPKINS
With pumpkin heads all peering, Is it not a fearsome sight? For the witching hour is nearing Of Hallowe'en midnight!
DESIGN COPYRIGHTED JOHN WINSCH, 1913.

HALLOWE'EN JOLLITY!
The solemn owl and the pumpkin gay Will dance all night till break of day, For this is Hallowe'en so jolly The time for fun and the night for folly!
DESIGN COPYRIGHTED JOHN WINSCH, 1913.

FRANK MILLER'S BLACKING

Unless otherwise noted, all antique paper ephemera items reproduced in this book were printed by the nineteenth-century color process of chromolithography.

Information about each item is arranged in the following order: type of item; title and/or description; size, where applicable; materials and printing method; artist, when known; lithographer, when known; date.

Descriptions read clockwise, beginning at the center top of each page.

Endsheets: Pages from an English scrap album, actual size; c1890.

P. 5: Stock advertising window card, imprinted "Kis-me Gum Co."; die cut, embossed easel back; 14.5"h x 13"w; c1900. Eyelet lace apron; c1890. **P. 6:** Foldout valentine; scraps, die cut, embossed, gilded; stiffened gauze, pleated silk, glitter; 5"h x 6⅜"w x 5"d; c1900. Hairpin, lace doily; c1900. Scraps (cherubs, roses), die cut, embossed; c1885. **P. 7:** Scrap (girl holding rose), die cut, embossed; c1880. **P. 8:** Scrap (flower wreaths), die cut, embossed; c1880. **P. 9:** Valentine; silk woven center, silvered paper lace; c1880. **P. 10:** Cameos; c1915. Scrap (hand with flowers), die cut, embossed; c1890. Salesman's sample cigar label; gilded and embossed; O.L. Schwencke Lithographic Co., New York; c1895. Mother-of-pearl pen with gold nib; c1890. Visiting card, c1890. **P. 11:** Trade card; "Celluloid Starch," die cut; c1890. **P. 12:** Calendar illustration, trimmed; c1900. **P. 13:** Scrap (children in garden); die cut, embossed; c1880. **P. 14:** Scrapbook, "Our Own Selections"; c1880. Uncut sheet of scrap, "Familiar Birds"; Mamelok & Sohne, Germany; c1890. Brass embossing die, "Julia Marlowe" cigar label; c1905. Original lithograph stones, "La Carolina," "Van Dam" cigar labels; Bavarian limestone; Van Dam stone, 9"h x 11"w x 2⅞"d, 27 pounds; George Schlegel Lithographer, New York; c1910. **P. 15:** Original watercolor art, "Persian Queen" cigar label; Henry Maier, artist (1884–1949). Original watercolor art, "Liberty Light" cigar label; American Lithograph Co.; by Henry Maier. Business card, Henry Maier; c1935. Original watercolor art, cigar label; Henry Maier; c1910.

HOME SWEET HOME

P. 16: Album card; c1885. Paper doll family, "Hood's Pills"; C.I. Hood & Co.; c1894. Scrap (dogs and cats on cushions), die cut, embossed; c1885. Valentine greeting (foldout birdcage); Raphael Tuck & Sons, Ltd., London; c1910. **P. 17:** Trade card, "Singer Manufacturing Co."; Caulon Printing, New York; c1890. Embroidered edging; c1870. Curtain tie-backs; c1910. Lamp prisms; c1880. Foldout Christmas greeting; c1900. Valentine; paper lace, applied scrap, handwritten inscription; English; Dobbs, Kidd & Co.; c1860. "Mechanical" trade card; opening card moves maid toward table; "H.J. Heinz Co."; c1895. **P. 18:** Commemorative card of Prince Albert and Queen Victoria's wedding; F. Boileau, artist; Summers and Smith, London; c1890. **P. 19:** Chromolithograph portraits, Queen Victoria and Prince Albert; c1885. Scrap (Queen Victoria), die cut, embossed; c1890. "Jubilee" 50th Anniversary pin; c1885. **P. 20:** Scraps (babies, children), die cut, embossed; c1880–1890. Miniature ceramic shoes; c1910. Baby rattle with bell; c1880. Silver cat-shaped baby rattle with mother-of-pearl and ivory; c1860. **P. 21:** Postcards, embossed; c1910. Scraps (stork, mother and child, little girl), die cut, embossed; c1890. Advertising bookmark, "Dr. D.B. Hand's Remedies for Children"; Stecher Lithography Co., Rochester; c1907. **P. 22:** Trade card, "Thomas Alva Edi-

son"; Leibig Company's Fleisch Extract, Germany; c1900. Trade card, "The Fireside Open-Front Stove," New York; c1890. Trade card, "Levering Coffee"; c1880. Pumpkin can label; Olney & Floyd; c1890. Soda label; c1910. Portrait pin; c1870. Scrap (girl with doll), die cut, embossed; c1890. **P. 23:** Shaped trade card; "Dougherty's New England Mince Meat"; c1891. Trade card, "Fleischmann & Company's compressed yeast"; c1890. Champagne label, die cut; c1890. Portrait pin; c1880–1910. Tomato can label; John A. Simpson, Label Printer, Baltimore; c1890. Trade card, "The New American Stove"; Weed Parsons & Co. Lithographers, Albany, N.Y.; c1885. Lift-up shaped trade card, "David's Prize Soap"; c1885. Shaped trade cards, "Clark's O.N.T. Spool Cotton Thread"; c1885. Portrait pin; c1880–1910. Windowshade pulls with amber beads; c1900. Metallic buttons; c1900. Sterling-silver thimble case; Unger Brothers; c1890. Silver thimble with cherubs; c1890. **P. 24:** Scrap (boy with rabbit), die cut, embossed; c1880. Litho, "Residence of C.M. Saxton, Esq., Orange, NJ"; The Calvert Litho Co., Detroit; c1884. Steel engraving, "Pa's Prodigies"; Lily M. Spencer, painter; J. Rogers, engraver; c1850. Scrap (girl with birdcage), die cut, embossed; c1880. Trade card, "The Prudential Insurance Company in America"; Brett Litho, New York; c1890. **P. 25:** Trade card, "Pike's Toothache Drops"; c1880. Trade card, "Rockaway Beach"; Donaldson Brothers Lithography, New York; c1880. Stock advertising calendar, imprinted "Foley's Family Pills"; c1900. Trade card, "Ayers Cathartic Pills"; c1885. **P. 26:** Illustration, Kate Greenaway, artist (1846–1901); c1890. "Miss Muffet's Birthday Party"; Maud Humphrey, artist (1868–1943); supplement to the *Chicago Daily Record-Herald*, Sunday, February 22, 1908. **P. 27:** Calendar illustrations, February, June, 1898; Maud Humphrey, artist; The Equitable Life Assurance Society of the U.S.; Frederick A. Stokes Lithography Co. Calendar illustrations, September and October, 1904; Maud Humphrey, artist; The Equitable Life Assurance Society of the U.S.; Gray Lithography Co., New York. **P. 28:** Advertising calendar; gilded and embossed, 15⅜"h x 11"w; c1910. **P. 29:** Scraps (children), die cut, embossed; c1880–1890. Flue cover; chromolithograph, glass, leaded edge; 9.5" diameter; c1900. **P. 30:** Portrait pin; c1885. Trade card advertising, "The Universal Wringer" verso; c1885. Pen, swan quill; c1880. Pen, flexible steel-tippen, wooden handle; c1890. Rewards of merit; c1840–1890. "Mechanical" novelty card; wheel changes blackboard picture; c1900. **P. 31:** Lead-pencil box label, gilded and embossed; c1900. Trade cards, "Henderson's Shoe School"; c1880.

S. & G. GUMP,
581 and 583 MARKET STREET
SAN FRANCISCO.

FULL STEAM AHEAD

P. 32: Flat Dresden ornament (camel); gold foil over paper, embossed, hand-colored; c1890. Cloth label (pelican); silver foil over paper, die cut, embossed; c1880. Cloth label in shape of fan; gold foil over paper, die cut, embossed, chromolithograph applied to center; c1885. Fancy box lid label; embossed, gilded border, chromolithograph mounted from behind; c1885. Flat Dresden ornament (giraffe); gold foil over paper, embossed, hand-colored; c1890. Friendship card; hand-drawn; c1860. Cloth label in shape of fan; gold and silver, die cut, embossed; c1885. **P. 33:** Brooch, carved ivory with Oriental motif; c1915. Scraps (Oriental figures), die cut, embossed; c1885. Brooch; ivory in shape of carved fan; c1890. Necklaces; carved ivory beads, smooth ivory beads, onyx spacers; c1900. Brooch; ivory, filigree and enamel; c1900. **P. 34:** Lover's greeting card, Vienna; c1820. Scraps, die cut, embossed; c1885. Stock beer poster (detail); full size 22"h x 15"w; c1900. Friendship greeting card, hand-colored; c1890. **P. 35:** Salesman's sample cigar label, "County Fair"; O.L. Schwencke Lithography, New York; c1890. Salesman's sample cigar label, "Club House"; gilded, embossed; O.L. Schwencke Lithography, New York; c1895. Cigar outside label, "Gold Hunter"; George Schlegel Lithographer, New York; c1898. **P. 36:** Scrap (coach-and-four), die cut, embossed; c1890. Dresden ornament (dog and trunk), silver foil over stamped cardboard, hand-painted; Germany; c1880. Scrap (horse-drawn carriage), die cut, embossed; c1890. Business cards; carriagemakers; c1880–1890. Trade card folder, "Columbus Buggy Co."; Henderson Achert-Krebs Lithography Co., Cincinnati; c1890. Dresden ornament (carriage), silver foil over stamped cardboard; Germany; c1890. **P. 37:** Scrap ("Safe Journey"), die cut, embossed; M. Priester Continental Printing Co., London; c1889. **P. 38:** Scrap (steam engine), die cut, embossed; c1885. Railroad ticket, Missouri Railroad; 1879. Salesman's sample cigar label and tag, "Dining Car"; George S. Harris & Sons Lithography, Philadelphia; c1885. Cast-iron toy engine; c1890. **P. 39:** Cigar outside label, "The Overland"; George Schlegel Lithographer, New York; c1898. Scrap, "New York Elevated"; die cut, embossed; c1890. **P. 40:** Dresden ornament (steamboat), silver foil over stamped cardboard; Germany; c1890. Trade card, "Thomas Clyde"; Iron Excursion Steamer; four-color wood engraving; 1886. Scrap (steamboat), die cut, embossed; c1890. Steamer timetable, New York City, Albany and Troy Dayline; 1878. **P. 41:** Ucut die-cut scrap sheet (shells); Raphael Tuck & Sons Ltd., London; c1890. Party favors: paper candy containers; c1910. Chromolithograph illustration; c1890. Miniature paper suitcases; c1900. Business card, Cunard Line; engraving; c1870. Dresden ornament (sailboat), silver foil over stamped cardboard; Germany; c1900. **P. 42:** Cloth label, Crystal Palace; c1860. Salesman's sample cigar label, "Liberty"; George S. Harris & Sons Lithography, Philadelphia; c1886. Salesman's sample cigar label, "World's Fair"; lithograph by Heppenheimer & Maurer, New York; c1876. Ticket, United States International Exhibition, Philadelphia; 1876. Salesman's sample cigar label, "Telephone"; George S. Harris & Son Lithography, Philadelphia; c1879. **P. 43:** Scrap, "Height of the Principal French and Foreign Monuments"; die cut, embossed; France; c1890. **P. 44:** Uncut sheet of scrap (children at beach), die cut, embossed; Raphael Tuck & Sons Ltd, London; c1890. Trade card, "Ayer's Hair Vigor"; c1885. Salesman's sample cigar label, "Surf Beauties"; Schumacher & Ettlinger Lithographers, New York; 1891. **P. 45:** Trade card, "Cowperthwait Furniture Company"; Charles Shields Sons Lithographers, New York; c1880. Trade card, "West Brighton Beach Hotel"; Donaldson Brothers Lithographers, New York; c1880. Trade card, "Steamship Columbia"; Ketterinus Lithographers, Philadelphia; c1885. **P. 46:** Scrap (elephant carrying children), die cut, embossed; c1890. **P. 47:** Scraps (wild animals), die cut, embossed; c1880–1890. Scrap (camel carrying children), die cut, embossed; c1890. **P. 48:** Box label, "The Bicycle Tobacco"; Schumacher & Ettlinger Lithographers, New York; 1869. Salesman's sample cigar label, "Speed King"; Schmidt & Co. Lithographers; c1910. **P. 49:** Trade card, "Columbia Bicycle"; c1880. **P. 50:** Business card, Palace Hotel; c1900. Scrap (boy on bicycle), die cut, embossed; c1885. Business card, Block Island; c1880. Business card, Spencer House; c1870. Flat Dresden ornament (bicycle); silver foil over embossed cardboard; Germany; c1890. Business card, Manitou House; c1870. Salesman's sample cigar label, "Royal Finish"; George S. Harris & Sons Lithographers, Philadelphia; c1895. Gold locket; c1890. Watch case; c1900. Gold stick pin; c1905. Cigar label, "Palace Court," San Francisco; gilded, embossed; George Schlegel Lithographer, New York; 1912. Gold handerkerchief or glove clip; c1890. Foldout valentine, "Love in a Motor"; Raphael Tuck & Sons Ltd., London; c1910. **P. 51:** Foldout Valentine; honeycomb, gilt paper, purple gelatin; c1910.

ALONG THE GARDEN PATH

P. 52: Stock calendar; die cut, gilded, embossed; c1905. **P. 54:** Scraps (dwarfs, floral oval), die cut, embossed; c1885. Lover's greeting card, "Freundschaftskarten"; "Constancy shall bring good fortune and abundance towards an excellent yield and guide your life garlanded with joy towards this reward"; embossed gold foil border, ornaments, mesh, applied scrap, hand-colored, motto; Vienna; c1820. Lover's greeting card, "Freundschaftskarten"; "If thou art as careful of our friendship as the flowers of this garden which charm every heart, then I will feel highly blessed"; embossed gold foil border, silver ornaments, mesh, applied die-cut leaves, flowers, fruit, ground hand-colored cardboard chips; Johann Endletzbergen, Vienna; c1820. Lover's greeting card, "Freundschaftskarten"; "Plant, in your life's garden, the loveliest roses, so you may weave garlands under tender roses"; die cut, with embossed gold ornaments, mesh, applied die-cut flowers, cloth flowers, hand-painted cherub; Vienna; c1820. Scraps (flowers in vases, flower seller), die cut, embossed; c1880–1895. Swan trinket box; Staffordshire; c1890. **P. 55:** Miniature glass tumbler; c1890. Scraps (flowers in glass, basket, vase), die cut, embossed; c1880–1890. Lamb; Staffordshire; c1890. **P. 56:** Dance program folder, "T.A. Holland's Juvenile Dancing Classes"; gilded paper lace, scrap center applied, tasseled cord with ivory-topped pencil, pull tab reveals three scenes; 1881. Dresden ornament (turtle); hand-painted, gold foil over stamped cardboard; Germany; c1900. Hand-painted porcelain pin; c1900. **P. 57:** Scrap (peacock feather fan), die cut, embossed; c1885. Dresden ornament (peacock), hand-painted, gold foil over stamped cardboard; Germany; c1900. Salesman's sample cigar label, gilded, embossed; O.L. Schwencke Lithography, New York; c1900. Dresden ornaments (fish), hand-painted, gold and silver foil over stamped cardboard; Germany; c1900. Trade card, "Metropolitan Life Insurance Company of New York"; 1886. Scrap (bird), die cut, embossed; c1885. Trade card, "Mexican Hammock;" Mayer, Merkel & Ottmann Lithography, New York; c1885. Trade card, "New Easy Lawn Mower"; J. Ottmann Lithography, New York; c1890. Seed catalog, back cover illustration; Peter Henderson & Co.; Gast Lithography and Engraving Co., New York; 1893. Dresden ornament (frog), gold foil over stamped cardboard, hand-painted; Germany; c1900. Scraps (owl, waterlilies), die cut, embossed; c1885. **P. 58:** Scrap (angels

around a cross), die cut, embossed; c1890. Devotional card; celluloid, printed in white, applied scrap with gold stamping; c1890. Scrap (white roses), die cut, embossed; c1885. Album card (angel); die cut, gilded, embossed; c1890. Portrait pin; paste and gunmetal chain; c1900. Floral Bible; silver; William Comyns, London; c1909. Handkerchief; c1910. Album card in shape of cross; c1900. Scrap (ivy cross), die cut, embossed; c1885. Confirmation card; embossed paper lace; c1909. **P. 59:** Scrap (cross with waterlily), die cut, embossed; c1885. Devotional card, "The Good Shepherd"; paper lace border surrounding gold embossed foil border; scraps applied on netting; c1885. Scraps (motto, "Trust in the Lord," floral crosses, angel with child), die cut, embossed; c1885. Hair jewelry; c1870. Sunday School card; applied scrap; Colton, Zahn & Roberts, New York; c1885. Page turner; mother-of-pearl, amethyst and silver; c1890. Prayerbook with silver cherub case; c1903. Scrap (cross of thorns with passion flowers), die cut, embossed; c1880–1890. **Pp. 60–61:** Scraps (flower fairies), die cut, embossed; c1885. **P. 62:** Original watercolor art, "Tiller" cigar label, Henry Maier, artist; c1905. Seed catalog back cover, "Burpee's Farm Annual"; Beatty & Votteler Lithographers, New York; 1889. Reply envelope; 1889. Trade card, "Vegetable Woman"; Parker & Wood Seed Store; Clay & Richmond Lithographers, Buffalo; c1885. Trade card, "Vegetable Man"; Holden & Robinson Seeds; Clay & Richmond Lithographers, Buffalo; c1885. Trade card, "Vegetable People"; Rice's Seeds; 1887. Seed catalog page, Mill's Seed House; three-color wood engraving; 1909. Seed catalog color plate (tomatoes and pole beans); "Burpee's Farm Annual"; 1890. Scrap (sunflower), die cut, embossed; c1885. Seed packets, "Burt's Seeds"; Genesee Valley Lithography Co., Rochester; 1916. **P. 63:** Scrap (poppies), die cut, embossed; c1885. Seed catalog pages, Currie Brothers; wood engraving; 1897. Cloth label; c1890. Cloth label; hand-colored; c1850. Trade card, "Champion Harvesting Machines"; G.H. Dunston Lithography, Buffalo; c1895. Scrap (sunflower), die cut, embossed; c1885. "Burpee's Farm Annual"; Stecher Lithography Co., Rochester; 1894. Seed packet with seeds, "Earliest White Bush Squash"; William Henry Maule Seedsmen; c1890. Store poster, Rice's Seeds; c1875. Store poster, Rice's Seeds; c1875. Order forms, Vick's Seeds; 1889. Store poster, Rice's Seeds; c1875. **P. 64:** Seed catalog, "Vick's Illustrated Floral Guide"; The Match Lithography Co., New York; 1889. Scrap (girl with flower), die cut, embossed; c1885. Miniature parasol; c1910. Seed catalog, "Vick's Illustrated Floral Guide"; J. Walton, artist; C.F. Muntz & Co. Lithographers, Rochester; 1873. **P. 65:** Scrap (girls with parasol), die cut, embossed; c1885. Seed catalog, Greene's Nursery Co.; Brett Lithography Co., New York; 1896. Scrap (girl

with flower), die cut, embossed; c1885. Seed catalog pages, "B.K. Bliss & Sons' Gardener's Almanac"; Clark W. Bryan & Co., Springfield; 1876. Scrap (gooseberries), die cut, embossed; c1885. **P. 66:** Needlework pattern, *Godey's Lady's Book*; 1861. Needlework patterns, *Peterson's Magazine*; 1874–1878. Album card, "God Bless Our Home"; c1885. **P. 67:** Needlework patterns, *Peterson's Magazine*; 1874–1878. Album card; die cut; c1885.

FASHIONABLE LADIES

P. 68: Stock calendar illustration; die cut, embossed; c1910. Ivory beads; c1900. **P. 69:** Scraps (flowers, birds), die cut, embossed; c1885. Cameo; c1905. Pearl necklace; c1925. Fabric flowers; c1930. **P. 70:** Toy sewing machine, tin; c1870. Toy flatirons; c1890. Fashion plate, "Winter Hats"; *The Delineator*; 1901. Dresden ornament (with thimble case), glazed die-cut paper, stamped silver and gold foil over cardboard; c1900. Stock calendar illustration; die cut, embossed, gilded, silver glitter; c1905. **P. 71:** Wall decoration, paper board; 9½" diameter; die cut, embossed and gilded; Ryland, artist; The N.K. Fairbank Co.; 1902. Cupid button; c1880. Gilt pin; c1910. **P. 72:** Scraps (fashionable ladies), die cut, embossed; c1880–1895. Scrap (boot with ice skate, flowers), die cut, embossed; c1885. **P. 73:** Scraps (fashionable ladies), die cut, embossed; c1880–1895). **P. 74:** Store window card (trimmed), "Hagan's Magnolia Balm"; Schumacher & Ettlinger Lithographers, New York; 1875. **P. 75:** Mourning cards; blank embossed; England; c1860. Molded horn brooch; c1860. Gutta-percha necklace with pendant; c1860. "Frozen Charlotte" china doll; c1860. Tiny china doll; c1850. Album card; c1885. "Myth" cameo, pinch back; c1880. Black background stock trade cards, various imprints; c1885. **P. 76:** Silk pin cushion; c1900. Hat pins and stick pin; c1880–1900. Label, "Rose Hair Oil"; c1860. Candy box labels; die cut, foil embossed, applied chromolithographs; c1885. Perfume label, "Extract Night Blooming Cereus"; c1860. Various cloth labels; die cut, silver and gold foil embossed, hand-colored, applied chromolithographs; c1850–1890. **P. 77:** Pin; paste and rolled gold; c1890. Box label, "Ladies' Heeled Boots"; die cut, gold embossed, applied scrap; c1875. Perfume label, "Eau de Lavande"; c1860. Salesman's sample cigar label, "Modern Kangaroo"; Heppenheimer & Maurer Lithographers, New York; 1877. Baxter prints, probably from cloth labels; England; c1850. Cloth label; embossed, gilded, applied Baxter print center; c1850. **P. 79:** Cloth label; embossed, gilded, applied Baxter print center; c1850. Baxter prints, probably from cloth labels; England; c1850. **P. 80:** Cigar label proof, "Vassar Girl"; George Schlegel Lithographer, New York; c1905. Beaded bag; c1890. Miniature hat and bag; c1980. Hat box label; c1870. Trade card, "Edwin C. Burt Fine Shoes"; 1881. Scrap (flower basket), die cut, embossed; c1885. Illustration of a huntress; c1895. Advertising novelty (woman with tennis racket); die cut, applied chromolithograph, paper honeycomb, satin ribbon, imprinted "Merry Christmas from the Lausset Street Lunch Basket" on bib front under homemade paper lace and scrap overlay; 1899. **P. 81:** Paper ornament (jointed doll); dressed in lace over crepe-paper with crepe-paper bows; c1895. Miniature doll and stroller; c1880. Stock advertising calendar (pad missing); die cut, embossed; c1900. Cigar label, "Texie"; Calvert Lithography Co., Detroit; 1898. **P. 82:** Stock calendar illustration; die cut, embossed, gilded; c1900. Foldout dimensional calendar, "Sweet Lilac"; die cut, embossed, gilded; 1904. Perfume labels; die cut, embossed, gilded; Lorenzy Palanca, Jean Giraud Fils, Victor Vaissier; Paris; c1900. Double heart pin; gilt, paste; c1910. Silver scent flask on chain; c1900. **P. 83:** Lace dresser scarf; c1920. Button; c1900. Cameos; c1860. Perfume labels; die cut, embossed and gilded; Lorenzy Palanca, Victor Vaissier; Paris; c1900. Mechanical advertising postcard folder; opening causes hand to powder face; Dresden face powder; 1911. **P. 84:** "Hidden name" visiting cards; applied die-cut scrap with caller's name underneath; c1885. **P. 85:** Bar soap, "Queen Beauty Toilet Soap"; 1905. Box label, "Kunkel's Magic Hair Dye"; 1874. Locket; gilt and enamel with ornate pin; c1910. Silver pin cushion; c1880. Stock trade card, imprinted "Nellie Allen, Milliner"; c1885. Scrap figures, die cut, embossed; c1885. Box label, "Queen Bess Corset"; c1880.

MANLY PURSUITS

P. 86: "Home Baseball Game"; McLaughlin Brothers, Inc., New York; 14¾"h x 14"w; wooden playing pieces, spinner; c1905. **P. 87:** Outside cigar label, "Hans Wagner" (Honus Wagner); George Schlegel Lithographer, New York; c1910. Scrap (baseball players), die cut, embossed; c1890. Original watercolor art, portrait of Charles Comiskey; John Fitz, artist; 1896. Miniature glove and ball; c1890. Trade card, "Emerson Piano Co."; c1890. **P. 88:** Cigar label, "Lord Broadway"; George Schlegel Lithographers, New York; c1900. Cane with gold head; c1890. Stick pins, scarab and glass; c1890. Calling cards; two with die-cut edges, beveled, gilded, applied miniature photographs; c1890. Dresden ornament (Greyhound dog); stamped cardboard, hand-painted; Germany; 1900. Silver cigar case; c1900. **P. 89:** Salesman's sample cigar label, "Smoking Car"; multicolor wood engraving; G.S. Harris & Son Lithography, Philadelphia; c1874. **Pp. 90–91:** Stock trade cards, various imprints; c1880–1890. Cigar label, "Merchant" (A.T. Stewart); George Schlegel Lithographer, New York; c1905. **P. 92:** Trade card folder (shown open and closed), "Oliver Chilled Plow Works"; Gies & Co., Buffalo; c1880. Salesman's sample cigar label, "Punch"; Cuba; c1875. **P. 93:** Cigar label, "Sunset Club"; c1910. Store window card, "Arthur Donaldson"; c1915. **P. 94:** Scrap (equestrian group), die cut, embossed; c1885. "Transformation" trade card, "Buckingham's Dye"; bottom folds down to reveal beard dyed black; c1880. Dresden ornament (jockey on jumping horse), silver foil over stamped cardboard, hand-painted figure; c1900. Box label, "Atlantic Collar"; c1870. **P. 95:** Catalog, sportsman's boots; c1910. Salesman's sample shoes; c1890. Miniature decoy; c1890. Trade card, "Clark's Mile-End Spool Cotton Thread"; Trautmann, Bailey & Blampey, New York; c1885. Dresden ornament (horse), silver foil over stamped cardboard; c1900. Scrap (equestrian figure), die cut, embossed; c1880. Doll's woolen gloves; c1880. Box label, "New York Hat Store"; c1880. Stock trade card, imprinted "D.A. Mariner, Practical Hatter"; J.M. Buffords Sons Lithography, Boston; c1880. Cloth label (jockey on horse), die cut, embossed, silver foil over paper; c1880. Black background calling card; c1885. Bottle label, "Bourbon Whiskey"; multicolor wood engraving; c1875. **P. 96:** Salesman's sample cigar label, "Centre Rush"; Louis E. Newman & Co. Lithographers, New York; c1895. Marbles; c1860–1910. Marble bag; c1890. Cigar label, "Newsboy Cigars"; Calvert Lithographic Co., Detroit; 1901. Trade card, Spencerian Steel Pens; c1885. Scrap (boy with dog), die cut, embossed; c1885. Outside cigar label, "Little Scout"; American Lithographic Co., New York; 1914. **P. 97:** Cigar label, "Shiner"; George Schlegel Lithographer, New York; c1900. Cigar box trim, "College Days"; George Schlegel Lithographer, New York; 1913. Paper box; applied label, "Empire Knife Works"; c1880. Pocket knife; c1880. Miniature razor and shaving mug; c1910. Cigar label, "College Days"; George

Schlegel Lithographer, New York; 1913. **P. 98:** Cigar label, "Sir Thomas Lipton"; George Schlegel Lithographer, New York; c1915. Salesman's sample cigar label; "On deck"; O.L. Schwencke Lithography, New York; c1895. **P. 99:** Salesman's sample cigar label, "Pretty Pilot" (detail); American Lithographic Co., New York; 1901. Salesman's sample cigar label, "Cup Defender"; Schmidt & Co. Lithographer, New York; 1895. **P. 100:** Salesman's sample cigar label, "Honest Labor"; O.L. Schwencke, Lithographer, New York; c1890. Cigar label, "Poet"; George Schlegel Lithographer, New York; c1900. Salesman's sample cigar label, "Home Pleasure"; O.L. Schwencke Lithographer, New York; c1895. **P. 101:** Scrap (man and dog) die cut, embossed; c1885. Advertising window card, "Standard Biscuits"; die cut, embossed; c1900. **P. 102:** Salesman's sample cigar label, "Rail Birds"; c1895. Salesman's sample cigar label, "Old Sports"; O.L. Schwencke Lithographer, New York; c1895. Salesman's sample cigar label, "The Crack Runner"; Louis E. Neuman & Co., New York; c1895. **P. 103:** Salesman's sample cigar label, "Try Me" (detail), William Steiner & Co. Lithographers, New York; c1900. Salesman's sample cigar label, "All for Luck"; c1895. Salesman's sample cigar label, "Lucky Spots " Krueger & Braun Lithographers, New York; c1895. **P. 104:** Lead soldier; c1910. Presidential pin-back button; c1910. Box label, lead soldiers; Germany; c1910. Trade card series, "Uniforms of the Army of the United States"; J&P Coat's Spool Cotton; G.H. Buek & Co. Lithographers; 1841–1851. Ribbon souvenir: Centennial of the United States; lithographed on silk; 1876. **P. 105:** Salesman's sample outside cigar label, "Military Brand"; Heppenheimer & Maurer Lithographers, New York; c1875. Salesman's sample outside label, "John Howard Payne"; Witsch & Schmitt Lithographers, New York; c1885. Badge holder; c1890. Ribbon, "The Star Spangled Banner"; woven silk; Warner Manufacturing Co., Paterson, N.J.; c1876. Cigar bands; c1900–1910. Trade card series, "Uniforms of the Army of the United States"; J&P Coat's Spool Cotton; G.H. Buek & Co. Lithographers; 1888–1893. Penpoint boxes; English; c1900. Silver brooch; c1910. "Uniforms of the Army of the United States"; 1872–1880. "Uniforms of the Army of the United States"; 1861–1866. Advertising novelty, "Our Navy Forever"; die cut, embossed, imprinted "Utica Cleansing Compound Co." verso; c1898. "Uniforms of the Army of the United States"; 1889–1890. Cigar label, "Rough Riders"; embossed, gilded; c1898. Cigar label, "Men of War"; George Schlegel Lithographer, New York; 1898.

ROMANTIC NOTIONS

P. 106: Valentines: Blue and gold paper lace; c1875. Gilded

paper lace scrap; center lifts to reveal second scene and motto; c1880. Gilded paper lace, paper wafer behind center; 1879. Paper lace gilded and stenciled, silk mesh center, applied green gauze leaves, flower scraps, hand-painted cherub die cut; c1855. Paper lace, foil leaves, scrap, hand-painted flower wreath, gold foil sheet behind; c1865. Chromolithograph, gilded, gold embossed vase scrap, hand-applied and painted flowers; c1860. Gilded paper lace, die-cut scrap applied on silk, hinged to reveal Valentine oracle with brass spinner; England; c1870. Silver and pale green paper lace; silver scrap, gathered silk netting oval, bound with silver wire, hand-cut and painted cupid; c1860. **P. 107:** Booklet, "The Lady's Own Valentine Writer"; 34 pp.; T.W. Strong, New York; 1860. Valentines: Silver paper lace, center scrap lifts to reveal sentiment; Whitney, maker; c1880. Embossed paper lace, applied scrap, glazed purple paper behind with sentiment gold imprinted; c1880. Paper lace, wood, applied scrap; center lifts to reveal gold embossed scrap, deep red paper behind; c1865. Green printed paper lace, applied scrap, paper wafer, yellow paper behind; Whitney, maker; c1870. Gilded paper lace, applied scrap; c1875. Heart-shaped, hand-colored, opens to form heart-shaped flower petals, each with embellished sentiments; c1850. "Valentine of True Love"; engraved; A. Kollner Lithography, Philadelphia; 1850. Paper lace, applied scrap, center figure lifts to reveal sentiment; c1875. Gilded cameo paper lace, Mossman, applied scrap, blue paper behind; c1875. Embossed paper lace, Windsor, gold foil frame, paper wafers; c1870. Booklet, "Ladies and Gentlemen's Valentine Writer"; 32 pp.; J.M. Fletcher, Nashua, N.H.; 1851. Valentines: Embossed, gilded, chromolithograph applied from behind cut-out opening; c1880. Gilded paper lace heart, Windsor, paper springs, applied scrap, cloth flowers, silver embossed; c1860. Gold embossed paper, scrap, colored paper; c1880. Decorative hanging die-cut trade card, "Fantail Pigeon Card"; McCullough Soap Co.'s Magnetic Soap, The Milwaukee Lithography & Engraving Co.; c1885. Lace shawl; c1900. **P. 108:** Foldout valentine (carriage); 8"h x 11½"w x 5½"d; Germany; c1905. Foldout valentine (cupid on bicycle driving flower cart); gold and silver embossed, applied scrap; c1890. **P. 109:** Foldout Christmas card (tower with romantic figures); 10"h x 4¼"w x 12"d; die cut, embossed, frosted, mica chips, pink gelatin film; hidden strings cause tower to rise when card unfolds; Germany; c1895. **P. 110:** Valentine; paper lace, silvered and hand-colored, applied silver foil, die-cut, embossed scrap, glass jewels, hand-colored scrap in center overlayed with mesh, handwritten sentiment; c1860. Silver heart charms; c1890. Cameo, paper lace with silver; c1870. Paper lace envelope; c1870. Silver heart trinket box; English; c1880. Silver stamp case; c1880. First-year special-delivery stamp; 1885. Valentine, cameo paper lace, applied die-cut leaves, motto, scrap; Dobbs Kidd & Co., 1866. Valentine envelope; lithographed in bronze, flourished Spencerian handwritten address; 1848. **P. 111:** Valentine envelope, embossed, postmarked February 14, 1857. Valentine envelope; lithographed in bronze, paper wafer seal; c1850. Brooch; silver and painted porcelain; c1910. Valentine; embossed paper lace, Mansell, watermarked "Towgood 1850," four layers of paper lace, gold and silver scrap embellishments, satin center, hand-painted cupid, applied die-cut and hand-painted wreath, hidden message under second and third layers, fourth layer lifts hand-cut "beehive" revealing color lithograph of two lovers; c1850. Envelope; embossed, gilded, folded certificate inside, applied mesh, silk ribbon, silver and gold embossed ornaments, blue foil; Germany; c1870. Valentine; "handkerchief" lace, hand-colored applied scrap, stenciling, circular mirror with cotton lace and pink satin ribbon; c1840–1850. French bisque doll; c1880. **P. 112:**

Scraps (cherubs), die cut, embossed; c1880–1890. Cigar label, "Love's Captive"; George Schlegel Lithographer, New York; c1895. Chromolithograph print; c1880. **P. 113:** Foldout valentine (boat with cherubs); gilded applied scraps; c1880. **P. 114:** "Mechanical" greeting card (shown closed and open); embossed gold, applied scrap, pull tab causes flower to open revealing child; Germany; c1880. **P. 115:** "Mechanical" greeting card (shown closed and open); embossed applied scrap, pull tab drops face of card to reveal three scenes, handwritten "Christmas" on back; c1880. "Mechanical" valentine card (shown closed and open); embossed with silver, silver foil, embossed scraps, folded pink tissue flower, pull tab activates unfolding of flower; c1870. **P. 116:** Painted porcelain pin; c1900. "Hidden name" visiting card; scrap lifts to reveal name; c1885. Scraps (forget-me-nots), die cut, embossed; c1880. Agent's sample book, visiting cards, Crown Card Co., Cadiz, Ohio; c1895. **P. 117:** Friendship cards, hand-colored; c1850. Painted porcelain pins; c1900. Battersea boxes; c1850. Miniature teacups; c1870. Scrap (envelope with birds, flowers), die cut, embossed; c1885. Miniature teapot; c1910. "Hidden name" visiting card; c1885. Scrap (two women), die cut, embossed; c1890. "Hidden name" visiting card; scrap lifts to reveal name; c1885. **P. 118:** Valentine fan; die cut, embossed, gilded, silk ribbon; Germany; c1912. Valentine; embossed, applied die-cut heart, multi-color wood engraving, heart folds out into four panels revealing wood engraved and hand-colored illustrations; c1875. Advertising paper doll, "Queen of Hearts"; Stollwerck's Breakfast Cocoa; c1900. Heart-shaped valentine card; die cut, embossed and gilded; c1910. "Mechanical" valentine; die cut and embossed, cupid folds out, pointer turns, easel back; c1910. **P. 119:** Escort cards; wood engravings; c1880. Salesman's sample cigar label, "Hearts"; George Schlegel Lithographer, New York; c1890. **P. 120:** Advertising almanac, "Rimmel's Perfumed Almanac of the Language of Flowers"; 3½"h x 2⅝"w; 10 pp.; London; 1863. **P. 121:** Album card; c1885. **P. 122:** Silk ribbon, "Stevensgraph"; woven design; T. Stevens, Coventry and London; c1880. Brooch; paste and metal; c1880. Gold fleur-de-lis pin; c1900. Enamel portrait pin; c1880. Chain, amethyst and metal; c1900. Ornate brooch, amethyst and gold; c1900. **P. 123:** Calendar illustration (trimmed), die cut and embossed; c1900. Embroidered dress collar, embellished with pearls; c1900. **P. 124:** Gold double heart pin; c1900. Postcard (lovers); embossed; Paul Finkenrath, Berlin; c1906–1909. Scrap (doves, flowers in basket), die cut, embossed; c1885. Heart pins; gilt and paste; c1900–1920. Foldout Jewish New Year card; die cut, embossed, glitter; Germany; c1895. Choker necklace; gilt with pearl separators; c1910. Scrap (doves, flowers in basket), die cut, embossed; c1885. **P. 125:** Postcards (lovers), embossed; Paul Finkenrath, Berlin; 1906–1909. Scrap (doves), die cut, embossed; c1885. Foldout Christmas card; die cut and embossed; Raphael Tuck & Sons, London; c1895. Scrap (doves), die cut, embossed; c1885. Scrap, die cut, embossed; c1885. Postcard ("A Fellow for every day in the week"); Germany; 1907.

DIVERSIONS

P. 126: Paperboard puppet, "Our friends the bears"; die cut, embossed, pull-cord activates arms; 11¼"h; Raphael Tuck & Sons, London; c1910. Stacking blocks, set of 12; chromolithographed paper over wood; Germany; c1910. Paperboard toys, "Animals and their riders" (clown riding cat, girl riding zebra); from a set of ten jointed, stand-up animals with riders; die cut, embossed; Raphael Tuck & Sons, London; c1910. Advertising novelty (space to imprint product name on rocker), girl and cat on horse; die cut, easel-back rocker; c1900. Scrap (dressed camel), die cut, embossed; c1880. **P. 127:** Scrap (dressed dog), die cut, embossed; c1880. Foldout calendar, "Dogs up to date"; die cut, embossed, radiator lifts up to reveal calendar; Raphael Tuck & Sons, London; 1908. Scraps (dressed dogs, rhino), die cut, embossed; c1880. Paperboard puppet, "The Jumbo family"; die cut, embossed, pull-cord on back to activate seesaw; Raphael Tuck & Sons, London; c1910. Advertising novelty (space to imprint product name on rocker); Mother Hubbard and Punch on a horse, die-cut, easel-back rocker; c1900. **P. 128:** Open scrapbook; 11¾"h x 8"w; c1880. Friendship autograph album; gold embossed; 1892. Scraps, die cut, embossed; c1880–1890. Glue pot, silver and crystal; c1880. Silver scissors; c1900. Uncut scrap sheet (beetles), die cut, embossed, gold stamped; Germany; c1880. Page turner, ivory and silver; c1880. **P. 129:** Uncut scrap sheet (cherubs and nineteenth century inventions); die cut, embossed; c1885. **P. 130:** Trade card, "Chase's Liquid Glue"; c1880. Uncut scrap sheet (cherubs); die cut, embossed, gilded; c1880. Uncut scrap sheet (charms); die cut, embossed; W. Hagelberd, London; c1890. Trade card, paper doll cut out, "Domestic Sewing Machine"; c1890. Uncut scrap sheet (garlands); die cut, embossed; c1880. Trunk and doll; c1980. Doll kitchen help; c1900. Miniature doll and bed; c1900. Cast iron dog; c1900. Commemorative name pin; c1850. Bisque twin dolls; c1920. Miniature crochet pram; c1900. Paper doll, "Courtly Beatrice"; designed by Marguerite McDonald; easel back, five dresses and hats in set (two shown); Raphael Tuck & Sons, London; 1894. Uncut scrap sheet (parrots); die cut, embossed; Littauer & Boysen, Berlin; c1890. **P. 131:** Paper doll, "Dolly Delight," No. 3 of "Our Pet Series of Dressing Dolls"; easel back, four dresses and hats (two shown); Raphael Tuck & Sons, London; 1895. French Bisque doll; c1890. Paper doll, "Dear Dorothy," Series 500 of "Dolls of all Seasons"; easel back, (four dresses and hats in set); Raphael Tuck & Sons, London; 1894. Uncut scrap sheet (flower baskets); die cut, embossed; M. Priester Continental Printing Co., London; c1888. **P. 132:** Dresden ornament (dirigible); silver foil over stamped cardboard; Germany; c1910. Cut-out sheets; model constructions, "Imagerie D'Epinal: Automobile, British Military Dirigible, Wright Brothers Biplane, Monoplane"; Pellerin & Co., France; c1910. **P. 133:** Cut-out sheets; model constructions, "Imagerie D'Epinal: 'Antoinette' Monoplane"; c1910. Dresden ornament (automobile); silver foil on stamped cardboard; Germany; c1910. Half-penny doll; c1890. **P. 134:** Game box, "Spear's Comical Tivoli Game"; clay marble rolling down chute animates clown; Spear Works, Bavaria; c1900. Scraps (clowns, circus performers), die cut, embossed; c1890. **P. 135:** Scrap (clowns), die cut, embossed; c1890. Petitpoint bag; c1870. **P. 136:** Game box label, "Illuminated Moving Pictures"; 14¾"h x 19½"w; French; c1900. **P. 137:** Jet beads and dress ornaments; c1870–1890. Half-penny dolls; c1890. Silver dollhouse chairs; c1890. **P. 138:** Invitation, "Grand Masquerade"; hand-colored lithograph; Lick House; Bancroft & Co. Lithographers; 1870. Scraps (masquerade figures), die-cut, embossed; c1880. Die-cut violin; c1890. Scraps (theatrical figures), die cut, embossed; c1890. Ticket, "Young Hennerchor Grand Annual Ball"; American Academy of Music; Theo Leonhart & Sons Lithographers; 1884. Postcards, "Carnival Series"; embossed; Raphael Tuck & Sons, London; 1908. Salesman's sample cigar label, "Sara Bernhardt"; Heppenheimer & Maurer Lithographers; c1878. **P. 139:** Curtain tie-back; c1910. Ticket, "Concert & Grand Ball"; Boston Coliseum; 1872. Trade card, "The Five Sisters Barrison"; Heymann & Schmidt Lithographers, Berlin; 1893. **Pp. 140–141:** Scrap (snow angel), die cut, embossed; c1890. Pop-up book spread, "A Visit to the Snow Queen's Palace"; *Peeps into Fairy Land*; Ernest Nister; c1900. **P. 142:** Postcard (Santa in his workshop); embossed; 1909. Stock advertising calendar illustration; 18"h x 15"w; c1900. **P. 143:** Children's book illustration; c1895. Children's book illustration, "On the Chimney Top"; *The Night Before Christmas*; McLoughlin Brothers, New York; 1896. **P. 144:** Metallic lace; c1880. Porcelain "snow babies"; c1920–1930. Flat Dresden ornament (Christmas tree); die cut, embossed, hand-painted scrap; c1890. Christmas tree ornament (celluloid shoe); c1890. Postcard (Santa portrait); International Art Publishing Co., New York; 1914. Foldout Christmas card (sleigh ride); W. Hagelberg, Berlin; c1890. Christmas tree ornament (Bunting tree); porcelain and cotton; c1900. Paper cornucopia c1900. Scrap (white-suited Santa, snow angel), die cut, embossed, frosted, mica chips; c1890. **P. 145:** Scrap, Raphael-style cherub; c1890. Scrap (snow child), die cut, embossed; c1890. Postcard (Santa in brown suit); gold stamped; Germany; 1909. Christmas tree ornament (Bunting tree); porcelain and cotton; c1900. Brooch, carved ivory; c1900. Scrap (snow angel), die cut, embossed, frosted, mica chips; c1890. Dresden ornament (star); gold foil over cardboard, embossed, stamped; Germany; c1900. Porcelain "snow babies"; c1920–1930. Scrap (white-suited Santa with children); die cut, embossed; c1890. Postcard (Santa with children around tree); Germany; c1905. Postcard (Christ child with snow angels in dirigible); Germany; c1910. **P. 146:** Heart-shaped valentine card; die cut, embossed, gilded; c1910. Scraps (cherub children), die cut, embossed; c1880. Celluloid bunny with cart; c1910. Black background stock trade card imprinted "Railroad Store"; c1880. Scraps (Christmas tree, family, angels, child, Santa face); die cut, embossed; c1880–1890. Christmas card (children around tree); L. Prang & Co., Boston; 1880. Scrap (green-suited Santa), die cut, embossed; c1885. **P. 147:** Scraps (fruit basket, eagle), die cut, embossed; c1885. Paperboard toys (rocker animal, turkey); die cut, embossed; rocker easel back; c1900. Wrappers, patriotic "snapping mottos" (popping sound when tab inside is pulled, small gifts released), chromolithograph of George Washington, ribbon, die-cut edging; boy with firecrackers, litho scrap applied to flat printed pattern, cut fringe; c1910. Trade card, "Frank Miller's Blacking"; J. Ottman Lithography; c1880. Postcards, Halloween; embossed; John Winsch; 1913. Black background stock card, hand-written inscription "Complimentary"; L. Prang & Co., Boston; 1876. **P. 148:** Foldout valentine (airplane with boy and girl); 6" high x 13" long x 15" wingspan; applied scrap, honeycomb tissue; Germany; c1920. **P. 149:** Stock trade card, ("this little piggie . . ."); imprinted "S&G Gump, San Francisco"; c1880. **Pp. 150–151:** Postcards (children on stuffed animals with wheeled platforms); A.&M.B., Germany; c1908. **P. 152:** Greeting card, Easter; c1885.